WITHOUT A SINGLE ANSWER

Poems on Contemporary Israel

Edited by Elaine Marcus Starkman
and Leah Schweitzer

JUDAH L. MAGNES MUSEUM
BERKELEY, CALIFORNIA

Cover painting: "And See the Land," by Anthony Dubovsky
Design: Sarah Levin and Sara Glaser
Typesetting: Wilsted & Taylor

Published by: The Judah L. Magnes Museum
2911 Russell Street, Berkeley, California 94705

ISBN: 0-943376-45-9
Library of Congress Catalog Card Number: 90-60828

Printed in the United States of America
10   9   8   7   6   5   4   3   2   1

For Leon, our children and our parents
For Norm and our family

In memory of Dr. Nancy Datan (1941–1987)
In memory of Dr. Bernie Vigod (1946–1988)

Acknowledgments

This book could not have come to life without the help of many colleagues and friends who believed in its merit. We owe our deep gratitude to Professor Stanley F. Chyet, Director of the Magnin School of Graduate Studies at Hebrew Union College, Los Angeles, who offered us his impeccable editorial talents and poetic sensibilities which sustained us throughout our work.

The following people advised us on our manuscript, watched it evolve, and gave us their invaluable suggestions: our thanks to Seymour Fromer, Paula Friedman, Rabbi Gordon Freeman, Roberta Kalechofsky, Sunny Solomon, Rebecca Fromer, Miriyam Glazer, Ernest Weiss, Jack Roth, and Consul General of Israel in Los Angeles, Eytan Bentsur. From inception to completion, each of them helped us develop our perceptions of what this book would ultimately become. We thank those who helped us in our search for material: Professor Dov Noy, Professor Warren Bargad, Julia Wolf Mazow, Myra Sklarew, Linda Zisquit, Estelle Gilson, and Chana Bloch. To Ren-na Blevins we express our sincere appreciation for her many long hours of help in putting this collection together. Her creativity, diligence, and patience were a gift to us. Our thanks to Sara Glaser and Sarah Levin for the design of this book and to Anthony Dubovsky for his artwork. Thanks to Sandra Hershkowitz, Merilyn Weiss, Florence Miller, and Nelda Cassuto who helped us proofread the manuscript; to Carole Alter, Sara Wallach, Herbert Gold, Hillel Halkin, Irena Narell, Professor William Brinner, Professor John Felstiner, Professor Milton Hindus, Joy Krauthammer, Larry Oliva, Susan Felix, Larry Brown, Zali Gurevitch, and the Creative Jewish Women's Alliance for their involvement in our work. A special thanks to Marcia Cohn Spiegel who brought us together so that this book could come to life—and to our husbands, Leon and Norm, whose common sense kept us going.

ELAINE STARKMAN
LEAH SCHWEITZER

Publisher's Note

The Judah Magnes Museum is pleased to participate in the publication of *WITHOUT A SINGLE ANSWER: Poems on Contemporary Israel*,
edited by Elaine M. Starkman and Leah Schweitzer, who conceived of
and brought together this important collection. The anthology which
they have created brings a new and enriched understanding to our
perceptions of Israel today.

This publication is a further expression of the Museum's growing
interest in the art of poetry. For the past three years, the Magnes has
sponsored the Anna Davidson Rosenberg Award for Poems on the
Jewish Experience, under the able direction of Paula N. Friedman,
who also served in a consultative capacity in the publication of this
volume. The response to the Rosenberg Award, with more than 900
entries from poets around the world, amply demonstrates the need
for this kind of cultural endeavor. It is our hope that the Museum will
be able to continue in this direction by providing a forum for poets
and by publishing poetry on Israel and other themes of Jewish
significance.

We are grateful to Lynda Levinson and the Max and Anna Levinson Foundation and to Leona Shapiro and the Leona R. Shapiro Publication Fund for helping to make this publication possible. We also
wish to acknowledge with gratitude the efforts of Sarah Levin and
Sara Glaser in the design and production of this handsome volume.
The book is wonderfully enhanced by the beautiful drawings of Anthony Dubovsky, to whom we are indebted.

Seymour Fromer
Director, Judah L. Magnes Museum
Berkeley, California
May 1990

Contents

Foreword

This anthology in many ways mirrors the vital love of and thirst for poetry evident in Israeli society. Aptly entitled "Without a Single Answer," the volume immerses the reader in a great variety of poetic voices, voices which derive from many different tongues, times, lands and experiences.

There is also a multiplicity of themes reflected in these poems: nature, love, work, death, celebration, places, cultures, philosophers, mythologies, ancestors, Messiah, ghosts, and the Holocaust. But the essential aura reflected here is the everyday experience. This is a collection of responses to the land, to its beauties, its hardships, its cities and settlements, its children, its passions and its disappointments.

There are questions, often oppositional, posed by the poets assembled: How do I feel about living/not living in Israel? How do I feel about coming to/leaving Israel? How do I feel about the land, the work in the kibbutz orchard or kitchen, my children growing up Israeli, the painful Palestinian issues, the constant Holocaust undertow, the sirens and shelters, the flowers and the blood? These are the questions and the voices of poets who are everyday people, who have everyday feelings, perceptions and visions. The poems embody a spectrum of personal experiences; they are prompted by personal reactions and are set in the boundless formats of poetic expression.

Many of the responses are to the experiences of place: Haifa, Tel Aviv, Ma'alot, Safed, the Jordan, Netanya—but most of all, Jerusalem. The presence of Jerusalem is felt throughout the collection. It is the locus of many emotions and motifs. It is the symbol of unity and division, the solidity of stone and the destruction by fire. It is the place of remembering, belonging, dying, loving, fearing, believing. It is the symbol of sacrifice and anger, morality and betrayal. It is at once the place of beggars and the pinnacle of dream. Much like Israel itself, Jerusalem enthralls, captivates, immerses, challenges, envelops and denies.

Although myth, symbol and allusion are not absent from this poetry, the overriding milieu is the life of a dweller in Israel. Even the poems by visitors, sojourners, or temporary residents give off the feeling of immersion in the land and its palpable—and often ambiguous—vitality. "In this country I cannot pretend innocence," says one poet. This is the essential emotion evoked in the volume: a sense of confronting the country, mulling it over, chewing on it, taking it in, spitting it out, contemplating it, perturbed, mystified, or captivated by it. As another poet puts it: once one has had the experience of Israel, "It's not easy to remain anonymous."

Personal experience is what this book is about. It is a book of irrepressible individual responses. It is a book which bares and confronts multifold feelings toward the looming presence and spirit of Israel today.

WARREN BARGAD
Director, Center for Jewish Studies
University of Florida, Gainesville

Preface

Since its establishment in May 1948, the State of Israel has been a magnet for headlines. The public life of the country is richly documented—wars, election campaigns, immigrant housing, religious demonstrations, counter-terrorism, archaeological digs, trials of Nazi war criminals, and bitter confrontations between Arabs and Jews and between Jews and Jews. Israel remains an international target blessed, but often enough cursed, by an overabundance of media coverage, with out-of-context images which must befuddle the casual observer.

Less well documented is the powerful influence the country exerts on the inner lives of both citizens and visitors. This influence, expressed in its belles lettres—fiction, drama, and particularly poetry—has not received the same attention that has been lavished on the public scene.

What we hope to offer here is a more balanced view of Israel's role in the modern imagination, a response expressed by variegated poetic voices. As Muriel Rukeyser wrote in *The Life of Poetry*, "The universe of poetry is the universe of emotional truth." That is what headlines seldom capture, but what this work means to illuminate.

Because we view these differing voices as facets of a unified concern—Israel—we have not separated them by country of origin or into distinctive volumes of English or Hebrew writing. Instead, we have placed Israeli, American, Canadian, and English poets in a blend that we consider unique.

These poetic voices assumed different meanings as the poems began to arrive. By January 1988, the celebratory, the narrative, the pictorial made way for a newer, more critical tone. These newer submissions expressed concern about the Arab uprisings in Gaza and the West Bank, a problem Israel inherited in 1967. As we read these poems we differentiated between polemics masquerading as poetry and honest poetic expression.

Those poems originally written in Hebrew, about a third of our collection, were made accessible to us through exceptional translators, often poets themselves who play a vital role in connecting the Diaspora with Israel. The translations have not lost any of their original zest which flows from the miraculous revival of Hebrew, reflecting both the colloquial tongue of today and the rich resonances of the biblical past. The juxtaposition of the two provides us with the vital energy of modern Hebrew verse today.

Our final selection was based on criteria that include the excellence of the poem, clarity of image, and economy of line. We chose poems for their strong sense of color, landscape or story—lyrical or rebellious poems that allow us to see the people and the country more clearly. Their form and theme are true to the characteristics of modern poetry—unembellished free verse with the poet's personal voice deeply felt. For the most part, the poems are passionate rather than measured responses to the profound questions Jews of the late twentieth century have had to confront regarding Israel.

Although we were aware of the enormous changes since Statehood, we were no less aware of the long tradition honoring poetry in Jewish experience. This tradition, particularly strong in Israel itself, has existed as far back as the Bible. Today, despite economic and political difficulties, poetry is a vital force in the lives of ordinary people. This phenomenon extends to Jews in the Diaspora, where certain poets have a need to demythologize Israel or redefine Zionism. Both Israeli and non-Israeli poets write about their sense of struggle with a Jewish nation that *must not* become merely another nation-state. Most of them express an intense relationship with the country, whether it be from an observation point on the border (Myra Sklarew), or from a Los Angeles Peace Now rally (Leah Schweitzer).

As a new collection, the work in *Without A Single Answer* is less sentimental and more encompassing than poems included in earlier anthologies on Israel. While we found expressions of persistent hope, pride, and idealism, we also found the pronouncement of despair and vulnerability, together with a sense of isolation and stark realism.

At the same time, these poems arouse quiet passions of daily life in tired cities, passions for the beauty of the land, and above all, passions crying out for the longing for peace and disparagement of war. Our contributors respond to the "special role" of Israel in the world as well as to their desire to depict a country like any other, one whose people make mistakes, become angry, or fall in love—often Diaspora Jews with Israelis—which has a significance of its own.

As Theodore Weiss, an American, writes:

> . . . the past [may be] oppressive [but]...
> you insist on your own loves and griefs,
> on living your own life, . . .
> the [clothes]lines flapping, not gaudy banners,
> but sheets and diapers, pants and slips,
> as if rehearsing private pleasures.

Or take, for example, three poems written by young women whose voices provide a feminist texture and message we cannot ignore: Kathryn Hellerstein's "Poem About Men," on American-Israeli cultural conflict and sexual mores, is so contemporary that it could only have been written by a woman of the 1980's; Avital Talmor's "Historical Boomerang" refuses to accept responsibility for the deeds of her pioneering forefathers; Irena Klepfisz's poem, "East Jerusalem, 1987: *Bet Shalom*," takes us one step further in her dialogue with Palestinian women.

We also thought it important to include a newer genre, poems by visitors, permanent or temporary residents who have become bonded with Israel. While many of our writers, such as Shirley Kaufman, are well-known poets, others, like Adina Hoffman, are newer writers. Kaufman, now a resident of Jerusalem for over fifteen years, asks for peaceful coexistence in "Meeting in Ramallah":

> what will become of your fast days
> and my atonement, what
> will become of us?

Adina Hoffman tries to put away her preconceptions in "Arriving":

> I am learning here to drink my coffee sweet
> and to pull cigarette smoke
> through my lips like string.

I must clean my lungs of
foreign air and breathe
what is here

And Nitza Agam is suddenly "thrust back there" when she meets
a Palestinian woman in San Francisco, a poignant example of how we
carry the Middle East and the history of Israel into our own backyard
9000 miles away.

The Holocaust is another strand which can never be separated
from the establishment of the State of Israel, nor can its literature be
ignored. It surfaces in such poems as Ruth Whitman's "Maria Olt"
and Richard Michelson's "For Forty Years," providing a link between
these monumental events. Pulitzer Prize poet Karl Shapiro's "Israel,"
written in 1948, and the late Marie Syrkin's "Protest Meeting" give us
the historical background which fortifies our understanding of Israel.

In contrast, there are poems on the simple pleasures of the moment: Miriam Grosman's "Netanya—Summer Morning" conveys images of early morning life seen from a balcony; Edmund Pennant's
"Storks" becomes more meaningful as subdued memories of a mas-
sacred Europe float through his mind. Along with these come the vi-
sionary poems of Berkeley "street-poet" Julia Vinograd, who visits
Jerusalem in her fantasies; Rachel Farchi Uziel's "Desecration of the
Sabbath" is full of extraordinary mysticism and ordinary irritation, a
part of Israeli life; Abba Kovner's symbolic wanderings stir a response
in us; the poems by Jay Shir and David Gershator recognize and re-
spect what is Christian and Arab in the land.

We hope that the plurality of voices in *Without A Single Answer* rep-
resents Israel not as an icon of the past or as a propaganda tool of the
present, but as a living nation among nations prepared to move into
the future with vision, strength, intelligence, and stability.

ELAINE STARKMAN
Walnut Creek, California
LEAH SCHWEITZER
Los Angeles, California
May 1990

Ten measures of beauty came down into the world; nine were taken by Jerusalem, one by the rest of the world.

TRACTATE KIDDUSHIN

Ten parts of suffering came down into the world; nine were taken by Jerusalem, one by the rest of the world.

AVOT D'RABBI NATAN

I
TO LIVE IN
THE LAND OF ISRAEL

HAIM GOURI

From "Gehazi Visions"

I live now in an ancient book.
I live now in the proper environment
which exports oranges and griefs
to half the world.

I live now in a white city
which burgeons with black dreams.
I live between rare imaginings
and absurd conditional sentences.

I move like a passing shadow
on a street unlike any other,
among hearts prepared for despondence,
toward the kingdom always to come.

I move between the saintly
and the lovesick.
I see men and women
back from the world to come.

Translated from the Hebrew by
Warren Bargad and Stanley F. Chyet

ARYEH SIVAN

To Live in the Land of Israel

In memory of Zvi Hurvitz
Pioneer, commander and bereaved father

To be cocked like a rifle, the hand
holding a revolver, to move
in strict closed rank, even after
the cheeks fill with dust

and the flesh goes, and the eyes can't
focus on the target.

There's a saying: a loaded revolver
will fire in the end. False.
In the Land of Israel anything can happen:
a broken firing pin, a rusty spring

or an unexpected cancellation order

like what happened to Abraham on Mount Moriah.

Translated from the Hebrew by Linda Zisquit

GRACE SCHULMAN

Jerusalem Street Talk

Outside, the vernacular is many languages.
Syllables hide under cypresses
that screen Mount Zion;
silent cries stir the Western Wall
where letters to God
shoot up like wildflowers
that break through stone.
Copts and Ethiopians
hardly speak to one another,
and sing to separate gods.
The people's harsh voices
strike steel.

ADINA HOFFMAN

Arriving

They do not believe
that I drink my coffee black.
When my friend laughed at me
she let her head tip
back like a china cream pitcher
pouring. Something about
vulnerable borders
life on constant call:
I am learning here to drink my coffee sweet
and to pull cigarette smoke
through my lips like string.
I must clean my lungs of
foreign air and breathe
what is here

Jerusalem 1987

ABBA KOVNER

The Hour's Late

Bare earth it is, the way to my love.
I come to her as to a rendezvous.
In silence I try to build on its ruins
a transparent city. To float houses astray
in two-lane streets. To restore their facades,
making them as orderly as crop rotation,
letting the sea burst inside into the tiny
square rooms to rinse the windows alternately
of frost buds and strips of sand,
as would a long relied-on housemaid. Already—

there's a highway.
A traffic light.
I can go now. Just let me hang
my hat on the swaying bough of an acacia, let me
fit my eyes with new traffic lights so they won't shut
at bad times. I've already tied my tie
to the neck of the wooden cock,
the tie with a pure gold pin
left me by my father. I'm still spreading out
my coat before the first policeman's dog
arrives on time running before his master. But my shoes
please let me leave my shoes
for the cat
until a better fairytale's found
for the children of the city
and you
you alone, little sister, I'll take with me
on my back. Carrying you across
my strip of bare earth.

Translated from the Hebrew by Warren Bargad and Stanley F. Chyet

MIRIAM GROSMAN

Summer Morning—Netanya

a starched,
embroidered
white linen
table cloth
covers our
breakfast table
on the *mirpeset*

across the street
Arab laborers have
already begun working—
later they will sit
in the shade and
eat watermelon
and bread

the stone tile floor
is cold
the presence of
heat lingers
heavy and damp
in the cool
morning air

a salad of cucumbers,
tomatoes, green peppers,
green olives in a separate dish,
leben, hard-boiled egg,
fresh bread, butter and jam,
nescafe with hot milk

I take out the garbage
in my thin cotton nightgown
stepping barefoot on
paving stones
sitting on sand—
I dodge large black ants
and the hungry gaze of
whining stray cats

the grapes on the ill-cared-for
vines are small and sour
the few lemons on the tree
in the side yard are
sour as well

Fania sprays cockroach killer
around the back porch
although it hasn't stopped
their ongoing
battle

she moistens stale bread
with water for the cats
although it hardly
satisfies their hunger

the heat rises
with the sun
and we go to the sea

the heat rises

Moving Lights

At the close of Independence Day 1972
a biplane rose
in the Tel-Aviv sky at dusk
and on its belly
moving lights flashed:

> For health and pleasure eat plenty of poultry
> Eat as you should with Deli Chicken Goods

In a small cafe
on Dizengoff between Nordau Boulevard
and the Northern Police station
(topped by a seven-branched *menorah* and a host of bulbs)
a handful of people sat
watching television
and between one tune and another
sipped a last cup of coffee
before sleep.

The neighborhood's dead silent,
last night's ruckus is over,
everything has returned to its place as expected:
the clientele to the cafe, the children home,
the flags to the closet and the worry to the heart;
the two regular whores to the entrance of Levinski's,
and the alarm clock to six o'clock.

A man and woman in their fifties, clad in pajamas
stand weighing the evening
on darkened balconies.
Three feet apart.
Yet they aren't speaking

or exchanging looks,
as though there is no common tongue
spoken in the land.

Oh, mighty Tel-Aviv,
darkened city feasting
a strange celebration of a nation's tongue-tied murmur:
oh television,
oh buses,
oh taxis,
oh Jews.

Translated from the Hebrew by Gabriel Levin

DAVID GERSHATOR

Jerusalem
In memory of Tchernikhovsky

Passover pagan
Easter heathen
Ramadan *kafir*
They come here for religion
I come here for wildflowers

We're worlds and words apart,
my flowers here before your
lawgivers, prophets, saviors

They follow their leaders
I follow the wildflowers
Each to his own shrines

Yehuda Amichai

A Pace Like That

I'm looking at the lemon tree I planted
a year ago. I would have needed a different pace, a slower one,
to observe the growth of its branches, its leaves as they open.
I want a pace of life like that.
Not the way you read a newspaper
but the way a child learns to read
or you quietly decipher the inscription on an ancient tombstone.

And what the Torah scroll does in the course of an entire year,
rolling its way from Genesis to the death of Moses,
I do each day in haste
or in sleepless nights, rolling from side to side.

The longer you live, the more people there are
who interpret your actions. It's like a worker
in a manhole: at the round opening above him
all those people stand giving free advice
and yelling out directions,
but he's all alone down there in the depths.

Translated from the Hebrew by Chana Bloch

JO-ANN MORT

In the Kinneret Cemetery

"Whither shall I go from the spirit?"

Psalms

In this country, even the ghosts have ghosts.
Here, the dead hold national congresses—
Moses Hess, Nachman Syrkin,
Ber Borochov, and lonely Rachel:
Thrown from her perfect landswell.
What good was a poet with poisoned lungs
in a land where revolutionaries were farmers,
dreamers of a modern day Eden?

O Rachel: Tell the ghosts,
the soldiers, the children.
Tell the seekers who drop pebbles
on your headstone, who sit between
your spirit and the river, who read
from the pages of your verse
stored in a vault by the sea.
Say what will become of us.
What will we become?

STEVE ROOD

Untitled

I love the clean
snap of mustard
stalks when they've dried
to blue tinder
Then, they're like ruins
from which all the thin
passions of politics
have run out.
There is only
the sound of the wind
and crack of a lintel
falling
every thousand years.

II
APPLES OF THE EARTH

MARIE SYRKIN

Protest Meeting

Remembering grim hands—fists, palms, arms—
I said, "I will not raise my hand
Not here, where cameras grind."
Remembering vows broken,
I said, "I will make no vow,
Not here, not anywhere."
Then the chant called:
"If I forget thee, O Jerusalem,"
And my hand rose,
Stronger than I;
And someone greater than I
Swore with my voice
Amid the other voices.

Oh, the centuries that lifted my hand,
All the hands!

KARL SHAPIRO

Israel

When I think of the liberation of Palestine,
When my eye conceives the great black English line
Spanning the world news of two thousand years,
My heart leaps forward like a hungry dog,
My heart is thrown back on its tangled chain,
My soul is hangdog in a Western chair.

When I think of the battle for Zion I hear
The drop of chains, the starting forth of feet
And I remain chained in a Western chair.
My blood beats like a bird against a wall,
I feel the weight of prisons in my skull
Falling away; my forebears stare through stone.

When I see the name of Israel high in print
The fences crumble in my flesh; I sink
Deep in a Western chair and rest my soul.
I look the stranger clear to the blue depths
Of his unclouded eye. I say my name
Aloud for the first time unconsciously.

Speak of the tillage of a million heads
No more. Speak of the evil myth no more
Of one who harried Jesus on his way
Saying, *Go faster*. Speak no more
Of the yellow badge, *secta nefaria*.
Speak the name only of the living land.

1948

ADA AHARONI

The Second Exodus

Today, I again bring my grain vessel
to the docks of your granary, father—
while breathing the wheat smells you loved,
me in Dagon Silo in Haifa,
you far away in Cairo.

Joseph in Egypt Land, Canaanite jugs,
ritual bronze sickles from temples,
crushing-stones, mill-stones and mortars—
all link me back to you
on old rusty scales

I remember your orange-beige office
in Cairo's Mouski,
with deaf Tohami weighing
the heavy sacks of flour and grain
on old rusty scales.

And me listening unaware
to the birds' chirped warning
on the beams of your ceiling:
"Wandering Jew, open your Jewish eyes,
you will soon have to spread your wings
again, and look for new nest."

Mighty Dagon's giant arms storing in bulk,
fill my own silo with tears
that you are not here with me
to view this wonder

deftly handling bread to Israel—
the land you so loved
but are not buried in.

For you dear father,
I plant today a garden of grain,
for you, who always taught us
how to sow.

The Field

We picked cotton in the Golan Heights in the middle of the day with relentless sun bearing over us, the bright glare piercing our eyes, the only shadows under the leaves of cotton plants and our own figures walking and bending over through the fields among the green rows picking weeds as heat dripped off our bodies the sun at its zenith by noon, we were given a break for fifteen minutes, "hafsaka" in the foreman's shack and a cup of thick turkish coffee then back to the fields the long rows and rows of green light shining off plants above the hard dry soil with occasional puddles of irrigated water, mirage-like in the profound heat and sunlight that had no intention of letting up all day, just one big light offered to us as we would serve it and the crops, bending to pull a weed and move on slowly, to conserve energy drained by the heat of the kibbutz sun.

GABRIEL PREIL

From Jerusalem, a First Poem

Under these historic skies
I am older than Abraham and his stars,
and I am the young father of the children
playing among pink trees.

On Alharizi Street on a violet afternoon,
such an hour of grace
gazes out of an arched frame
as sometimes whispered to the prophet
weary of fires,
who dreamed of a village
cool among the stars.

Translated from the Hebrew by Robert Friend

ASHER REICH

Haifa in Winter

Haifa in winter is a Japanese woodcut.
There rainsilk awaits me, the softest of rains.
The shadow moth sleeps in the damp of the bushes,
and from the dreampuddles a mist slowly rises.
With the delight of clouds, Haifa in winter floats in the air,
and the horizon is sometimes a rice-paper sail.
Then like a wound in the belly of the city
—the sun-stained evening.

Translated from the Hebrew by Karen Alkalay-Gut

DINA ELENBOGEN

Apples of the Earth

I.

Everyone else is peeling onions
and I can't stop crying, can't
remember what I dreamt last night.
Muhammed shows me his card, tries
to tell me he's a Jew, lists
all of the serious holidays.
Shoshana shows me which shelves
to clean, which soap. I lift
a frying pan from the darkest corner.
The rust on my palm says maybe
the last time someone fried an egg
was the day we captured Bethlehem,
or the month fifteen of us
never came home. It's peaceful now.
The rattling windows just mean a plane
passes faster than the speed of sound.

II.

The Arabs are building another room.
The German guests eat strudel, the Koreans, green
melon, the Americans eat without trays.
Tamarah sings in Spanish and Hebrew
about horses and rivers in Brazil.
Sarinah and I dream of ski lodges in Aspen
and Vermont while we pick mint leaves
for our tea. I cut to the core
of the apple, the toughest but sweetest part.
The others drink coffee black, two lumps
of sugar.

III.

My hands are no longer my own.
How many potatoes have I peeled,
how many bruises have I carved
away, tossed in the bin.
In this language they are called
Apples of the Earth.
I sing the old songs and time goes quickly.
Amnon makes cat sounds.
Why doesn't someone let them in?
Doesn't anyone think the cats are hungry
just because they beg? Doesn't anyone think
I too want tea with mint just because I didn't ask?

LUCILLE DAY

Near Kibbutz Nir David

The oleanders are pink
or else white. They might
be painted on teacups, but toss
quietly beside a pool
rimmed by pale Roman stones.
The water, very blue and cold,
holds the sky.

People on the grass:
lovers, an Arab family,
a curly-haired boy, chased
by someone's black dog.

A plastic bag and two cans
float in the pool, relics
joining crude tools,
pottery shards, bits
of cloth in a universe
where molten stars move
in all directions.

SUSAN DICKMAN

In Wadi Ara

We ride like ghosts
in a silent ship through
the body of your land,
the land you have planted
yourselves in, winding the
stone roots of olive trees
around your legs like anchors
in the deep deep soil of earth
and death.

There are no lights
but the light of our faces.
We shine like open windows,
each drawn breath
caught like silence
from the fear in our hearts.

The gas tank is full
and our map is drawn
like fire through the night.
Behind our eyes
we see the road winding
its way to the sea
but the sea is a dream
now, as is the dream
of peace that lies burning
on the ground,
like the forests that
have burned for days,
acres of pine turned to ash.

Your homes glow like messages
from a faraway place.
Each darkened window is a word,
each vine and tree a voice
that speaks, but its language
is the language of wind
and stone and is nothing
but a whisper by the time
it crosses the long road
of wandering and reaches
our waiting ears.

We cannot hear you
anyway. Our car wheels send dirt
spinning backwards as we ride,
someone's voice on the radio is
pulling us away
from your road,
turning our eyes from the closed
night that holds only stars and
stones and houses that sit on hills
and breathe the air of a
thousand long years.

1988

Yehuda Amichai

Love of the Land

And the land is divided
into districts of memory and regions of hope,
And the residents mingle with each other,
like people returning from a wedding
with those returning from a funeral.

And the land isn't divided into war zones and peace zones.
And whoever digs a trench against cannon shells,
will return and lie in it with his girl,
if he lives till peace comes.

And the land is pretty.
Even surrounding enemies decorate it
with weapons shining in the sun
like beads on a neck.

And the land's a package-land:
and it's well-tied and everything is in it,
and it's tightly bound
and the strings sometimes hurt.

The land is very small,
and I can contain it inside me.
The erosion of the land also erodes my rest
and the level of the Kinneret is always on my mind.
Therefore I am able to feel it entirely
by shutting an eye: sea-valley-mountain.
And therefore I am able to remember
all that's happened in it
at once, like a person remembering
his entire life at the moment of death.

Translated from the Hebrew by Linda Zisquit

III
NO POCKETS FOR CHILDREN

RUTH BEKER

No Pockets for Children

One bald morning
screeching against the early
white sun like hysterical birds,
the sirens will start,
and I shall have to run
with my children to the shelter, the room
set off in my house
for keeping death at bay
with drums going instead
of my heart.

The children are waiting.
The alarms are ringing.
What shall I do?
I can't bury them in the ground
and pick them up whole and new again
in the spring. I can't sew them back
inside me until the all-clear sounds.
Where should I take them?
The shelter is only a shelter in peace,
for storing things;
it can't keep out war.

Maybe God has pockets somewhere for
storing children, but it's getting late,
and I haven't found them yet.
Where can I hide my children
before the earth throws them up
between the first siren and the last?

ELLIE HENKIND KATZ

A Child Is Sick in the Night

A child is sick in the night.
The mother weighs all possibilities.
Life and death are much more a question
in the impenetrable dark.
Shamelessly she wraps her baby and flies
to the Holy City.

The highway is strewn with black-coated men
whose garb announces the degree
of their God connections.
They also need to get to the Holy City.

"Can we fly together in the night?"
they ask.

"Will you pray for my sick child?"

"What is the child's name and
what is yours? We need these
facts to plug into our holy
incantations."

And when they come to their word for God
they wail the holy name, thousands of years old,
the ancient name.

The mother is struck by the blessedness
She silently weeps her prayers in her language.

MADELINE TIGER

Your Hand
for my son in Israel

Your hand covers the map,
Randall, you are gunning
life down, to live

"L' Chaim"
Having chosen to fight
among those who call
for you to be among them
who call themselves
"The Chosen," for suffering
for extending the green
orchards across the desert
Your hand
enlarges, you have learned
how to fix the machine
on the pipeline, to water
fields of avocado, flowering
broccoli, rhubarb, cabbage and
the curling lettuce; you brought
force, your own stream of
adrenalin and good will
to the earth you walked, learning
to plow and till and tend; to harvest
and pack fruits for market
You earned
your own keep, son,
and a pride in your arms

How far away you went
with your head full of tunes
and your heart—so sad, so hopeful,

so young—pounding
at the gates of the cities
impenetrable to your simple demands

There were no ears in the whole world
wide enough for your song, so
you had to become huge, all brawn
and wield combine, tractor, pipe, hose, gun
It comes to the gun
to the gun
in your great hand across the world
and the woman who bore you at Fort Sill
has to understand
her trickle of milk made you so tame
you had to reach beyond
the prayer of your name
to scoop up oceans in your cupped palm
to dog the desert and valley and plain

You needed, to be sure, to become
so big and tough and true
to one definition of you
that your little monkey hand grew
to encompass continents until it could
cover the whole globe—oceans/land—
Your advancing hand can protect you
from all evil, now, and all pain,
even the pain you said,
speaking of chains, that your mother began

E. M. Solowey

Winter Interlude

There is no soil outside my window
Only fissured stone
But the acacia tree seems healthy enough
It took root somehow
In a pocket of grit or sand
And pushed down into the flawed rock

My older son sits at the table
Doing his homework
Listening to the storm
He never speaks to me in English
Unless I offer him outrageous bribes.

My younger son runs to me for comfort
A falling block
Has pinched his small red hand
"Ai, ai, ai," he cries
He even weeps in an alien tongue

The tree is twisted, gnarled, thickened
I take the younger one on my lap
And hold him against me
As he cries easy baby tears
I can see the wind in the branches of the thorn trees
The wind blows
The tree grows
The rock splits apart
And the tree survives

JOEL ROSENBERG

A Letter from the Mayor about Packages

Dear Children:

I, the mayor, celebrate with you
the opening of a year of study,
and I wish you all success.

I have something to ask of you:
when you are riding in a bus,
or playing in a schoolyard,
or enjoying a movie,
please be careful
not to touch a package,
or a box, or any other thing
that isn't yours.
These things are liable
to be very dangerous.

If you discover
some belonging that's suspicious,
get away from it,
and call one of your parents,
or a bus driver or teacher,
or a counselor, or any grown-up
who can summon the police.

I beg of you,
please be alert and careful.

Yours in blessing,
Teddy Kolleck
City chief

Adapted from the Hebrew

MORRIE WARSHAWSKI

A Lover So Deep

The girls on the West Bank are
easy. They have stones for eyes.
They glance to the East and back to
the West. Nothing lies before them.
Nothing lies between them. They
sift sand between their fingers and
keep a straight back. They come
in all sizes. With flat sandalled
feet. And long long hair. Hair
that crosses the border between
here and there. It makes
a short brittle bridge
that only ants can cross. It
arches high in the dry breeze
above this plateau and that
plateau like a puffed chest
during an argument when the
throat is locked in rage and
teeth are clenched and the
heart is racing faster and
faster. So fast the little
tornado that forgot its father
skips through the dark bedrooms
of our dark West Bank girls tattooing
a cheek a forehead a lip swirling
the dark deeper and deeper
than a father or a son or even
a lover. So deep.

DINA ELENBOGEN

Maalot Cafe 9:00 A.M.

When the news comes on
the parrot chatters like mad
from his cage, digesting each word
in his narrow throat, while I take down
tea with *sheeba*, sweet wafers and Time.
Twelve of us taken today,
just over the border.
I have come here from the school
where Ethiopian children can't learn
my language but repeat all the sounds.
Even in this fog a car starts up.
We've lost the view of the mountains
but can hear planes whiz by
on their way to Lebanon.
When the news is over and the music
comes on, the parrot is silent.
I return to school breathless.

DAHLIA RAVIKOVITCH

Stones

Stones are *stones*.
Why did you say *stones*?
Why did you throw *stones*?
Why are you standing here, child?
What's got into you to throw *stones* at soldiers?
Why aren't you afraid?
Why aren't you worried, fearful for the future?
Why did you say *stones*?
Why do you have only *stones* in your head
and in your hands?
How swift-footed you are
and what are you getting at
with *stones*?
Now we said *stones*.
A child of seven, ten, nine, twelve
all throwing *stones*.
Approaching in a frontal column from the alleyways
with full hands,
a light and cheerful body,
all they have in their head is *stones*.
And there is much rejoicing,
perhaps they'll even manage to escape
and vanish like grasshoppers into hidden doorways
and this will be the day
Allah is great for them
a day of *stones*.
Between arrest and arrest
perhaps a clubbing,
perhaps even a wounded head
a hand broken

everything's possible for them.
Stones, stones, stones, stones.
Children, children, children, children,
come back home, children
how can you live without rest?

Translated from the Hebrew by Linda Zisquit

IV
JOURNEY TO THE CENTER
OF THE WORLD

JO MILGROM

Mobius-Trip

You shall take the fruit of a beautiful tree
                    Leviticus 23:40

Never mind the usual souvenirs,
olivewood camels and embossed silver prayerbooks
I want the real fruit of the Land
Manna
or some other mythic elixir
to nourish me in the long and hungry exile.

Sonja used to bring back Osem soup nuts
and Telma's fluffy kneidl mix.
Me, I have a thing for prune jam in leben
and those fat Arab raisins with seeds like nuts.

Tonight
Facing my yawning suitcase
a dilemma of different sorts
seeks its resolution.
It's about my tree of life.
Again.

Do I leave it here, in this home
planted in my newly plastered painted watered
navel of the earth
My portable axis mundi, rooted in me
and wiring my heart to heaven
wherever I may be.

I think I better take it with—
It is my compassionate balancing pole

as I wire-walk the contours
of perpetual departures
and arrivals.

LINDA PASTAN

Mosaic

1. The Sacrifice

> On this tile
> the knife
> like a sickle-moon hangs
> in the painted air
> as if it had learned a dance
> of its own,
> the way the boy has
> among the vivid
> breakable flowers,
> the way Abraham has
> among the boulders,
> his two feet heavy as stones.

2. Near Sinai

> God's hand here
> is the size of a tiny cloud,
> and the wordless tablets
> he holds out
> curve like the temple doors.
> Moses, reaching up
> must see on their empty surface
> laws chiseled in his mind
> by the persistent wind
> of the desert, by wind
> in the bulrushes.

3. The Flight into Egypt

> We know
> by the halos
> that circle these heads

like rings around planets
that the small donkey
has carried his burden
away from the thunder
of the Old Testament
into the lightning
of the New.

4. At the Armenian Tile Shop

Under the bright glazes
Esau watches Jacob,
Cain watches Abel.
With the same heavy eyes
the tilemaker's Arab assistant
watches me,
all of us wondering
why for every pair
there is just one
blessing.

SHULAMITH CAINE

Ibn Gabirol in Tel Aviv

Old poet friend!
How good to meet again.
Last time, in Malaga, it was by chance,
You, in that stumble-bum park
Surrounded by ragged, red-eyed loafers
Drunk before mid-day.
I looked away and hurried on.

And now we meet again,
Though some things have changed in the translation.
Here, a main drag in your honor,
With pricey shops, outdoor cafes,
Where mini-skirted flirts,
Like black-hatted Hassidim,
Swear by their thighs.

Last night the moon was a Moor's carved scimitar
And the sky his wind-blown velvet cape.
The flowers on Habima's plaza, jasmine, rose and lily,
Were perfumes of a Spanish garden.
"To life!" I murmured, raising high my cup,
And mused on dreams of golden times
When califs nibbled on grapes and figs,
And poets, like larks, sang rapturous lyrics of praise.

JOEL ROSENBERG

From "Journey to the Center of the World"

A meditation at the gate of sleep:
on stones and fire,
and the lack of middle ground.

The city's stones have soaked up olive vapor
from the first of days, from commerce
of the fathers and their foes. Mute, dark,
dreamlike drops of olive light unkindled,
like a wave of convoys
on the Paratroopers' Avenue,
that disappears into the night,
and leaves its seal of green-gray light.

Like iron wine inside a flask.
Like fire waiting to be summoned out.
Someday, the olive presses on King David Road
will overflow their fumes.

Then fire,
like a sudden extra breath at sleep's threshold,
will go forth, fire rising on an oil lamp.
Fire dwelling in the heart of prayer.
Fire haloes on the crests
of seven hills. A fire on the tongues
of lovers. Fire in the speech
of seventy nations. Fire in these walls,

born of the friction of our hopes
and scuffings of the body
moved in prayer. A fire lighting up
the Mount of Olives, kindling
all the trees like Sabbath wicks.

MOSHE DOR

Crossing the River

Today we cross the river. Even those who walk on foot won't find it difficult. Summer. The waters have greatly receded and each cattail poking out of the mud is also mirrored in the shimmering haze. First march the priests, prophets, soothsayers, the presidents of the tribes. Then family leaders, their kin, the slaves, the sheep and cattle. This is the river, dark and green. Guide books call it *Yarden*, *El-Urdan*, *le Jourdain*, *Jordan*, and it is written it serves as the gate to the promised land. Surely the books are right. This morning, moving slowly from east to west, we saw nomads track us on the opposite bank, galloping back and forth, brandishing thin lances made of reed. Immediately the priests held high the Tablets of Covenant. The nomads vanished. Perhaps they were only a mirage. Then we were given the signal to cross the holy waters.

Translated from the Hebrew by Barbara Goldberg

Marcia Falk

Dead Sea

In the middle of July at the bottom of the middle of the world,
water turns to salt
that floats like frozen waves: a petrified ocean.

Below the white horizon lies a still and perfect blue;
above it, the same still blue;
for miles around, a blue dome stopping time.

Beneath yellow parasols, bathers lean into the flat blue air—
blue so hot it is almost yellow—
and their bodies soak up sky the way salt soaks up the sea,
soaks it dry as bones,
until the sea is a sea of white bones floating on sky.

You can walk into the sea and keep walking: you will not drown;
but if you cut your foot on a salt-rock, the sea will suck the wound,
turning it into a white flower of pain,
which, like desire, will be fickle and brief:

you fill desire like a wound with balm and the wound heals over
and the skin is new and needs nothing more until bruised again.

Sometimes the mind alone keeps alive pain or desire—
as when a gesture,
such as the way a loved one throws back his hair,
embeds in the mind like a fossil
and the mind sucks the sweet imagined marrow—

the way birds skimming the salt-white water with their red-tipped wings
keep alive an ancient longing for wind.

DAHLIA RAVIKOVITCH

The Horns of Hittin*

In the morning strange ships appeared on the sea,
prow and stern
in the ancient fashion.
In the eleventh century
columns of crusader ships sailed off,
kings and rabble.
Crates of gold and plunder lay around in the ports,
ships of gold,
piers of gold.
The sun lit marvelous flames in them,
burning forests.
When the sun dazzled and the waves rocked,
their hearts went out to Byzantium.
How cruel and naive the crusaders were.
They plundered everything.

A boundless terror seized the villagers.
Their daughters were carried off,
blue-eyed grandsons were born to them
in shame.
No one spared their honor.

Slender-necked ships set sail for Egypt.
The magnificent troops marched on Acre,
a lightning force.
Each of them a swift knight bearing
the Bishop's blessing.
A great flock of
wolves.

*The Horns of Hittin: site of a celebrated battle in which Saladin decisively
defeated the Crusader armies in 1187.

How their blue eyes shone
when they saw the palm trees sway in the wind.
How they soiled their beards with spittle
when they dragged women into the brush.
They built many fortresses,
snipers' towers, ramparts of basalt.
Their bastards in the villages, now grown up,
marvelled at them.

In the twelfth century, the Marquis of Montfort
began to fail.
The winds of Galilee whistled over his gloomy fortress.
A curving scimitar burst from the East
like a jester's staff.
Saladin, in gaudy colors, advanced from the East.
With the horns of a wild beast
he gored them hip and thigh,
that infidel dog:
Saladin
did them in
at the Horns of Hittin.

No kingdom remained to them,
no life eternal,
no Jerusalem.
How cruel and naive the crusaders were.
They plundered everything.

Translated from the Hebrew by Chana Bloch and Ariel Bloch

ANTHONY RUDOLF

Ashkelon

In the space of time
we found

a bone
with a flower
growing out of it

a decapitated
terra cotta virgin
lying between
a coffin-nail
and a column of ants

the wedding-
ring of a Philistine
by a heavy
eucalyptus tree

a tiny obol
a bit of glass
the handle of a jug
a broken plate

ruined mosaics
shattered marble columns
and a sheikh's tomb

mezuzas of a sought past

two amorous lizards
embraced in the sands

it was raining
we made
a fire on
the beach the flames
survived the rain
and the meal we cooked was good
after we had eaten
we smothered the flames with sand
some charred egg-shells
and *matso* crumbs remained
they can't
have lasted long

MOSHE DOR

Excavations

The sky has turned into an iron dome.
Fierce gales drive from west to east, harbingers
of beautiful murderous Europe. Anxiously
we searched the armored horizon for banners
of the new crusaders. Then we resumed
our dig in the hard soil for shards
of history, coins for testimony, sarcophagi
whose bones we prize, confirming
covenants, for the sake of the future.

Translated from the Hebrew by Barbara Goldberg

CHAYYM ZELDIS

Autumn in Shomron

Autumn comes to Shomron
Shyly:
Only soft winds blow.
Jade-backed frogs topple into carp-ponds
That are as still as glass;
In the meadows, the cows stand motionless,
Gleaming like porcelain;
And the sheep, chalk-white, file slowly
Across the fields of mown oats and rye:
Then one day
Like great nets, the returning flocks of starlings
Billow in a moody sky.

Autumn comes to Shomron
Softly:
Only shy winds blow.
But to the east, the mountains burn darkly
And cast their shadows long;
And clouds pile up like haystacks in the winey
Evening light;
And whitecaps flash upon the sea,
Like horses' manes;
And in the dimming hush of the orange groves,
The leaves touch, each to each,
Thirsty
For jeweled autumn rains.

REVA SHARON

Covenant

Here where the passionate sun
burns over the hills illuminating
the vanished city of David
and the enduring Western Wall
where stone is the architecture
of loss and promise
and ancient olive trees
sustain their green intensely

Here where wind blows over
Gehenna carrying the wilderness
dust through the Gates
and down the cobbled
alleys into windows
and doorways and
the resurrected heart-
beat of the Cardo

Here where Rachel's tears
and the yearnings of exiles
fall with the rain
where the Lion of Judah
roars in the thunder
for generations
whose spilled blood
rusts the clay of the world

Here where goats are tended
on the hillsides
and here where Isaac
was spared
where morning sings

in the minor key of elegies
and gold twilight burnishes
sonatas in houses of stone

Here where the unsolvable
riddle of being
roots me
in this city that rises
where light and dust and wind
are fused to salt and bones and song
Here I will return and write
my name in Jerusalem dust

V

OF TWO LANGUAGES

JOAN ZIA KAHN

The Lion Whose Mane I Groom

The Lion of Judah
comes in all sizes and shapes,
speaks many languages—
surprises us every so often

I met him in a public library
in New York City, learning Arabic
from a record.

I bumped into him in Amsterdam
in a macrobiotic restaurant
eating a peanut/rice dish.

His Subaru hit mine on the Tel Aviv-Haifa
highway and he proceeded to curse
at me.

We study chemistry and modern Hebrew poetry
together at the university
share coffee and politics.

He has a ruddy face, sad eyes
wider than six-lane highways
and a great sense of humor.

One day the Lion of Judah
invited me into his world
and ever since then,
I've been unable to leave.

BERT MEYERS

When I Came to Israel

I saw my daughter
when I came to Israel.
She sat between its wars
by a soldier on a hill.

Stones and olive trees
and the bright air all around . . .
So many stones! like stars
painted yellow and brown.

Suddenly, my son appeared,
carrying on his back
the soft horizon
like a huge, blue knapsack.

He strode from a field
and lifted me,
the way a young cliff
lifts the grey-haired sea.

My little father, he said,
at last you're here.
The fields, the orchards,
everything seemed so clear.

Then my daughter ran
down down the hillside,
excited like a stream.
She called me; and I cried.

But my wife was a dove
in the wailing wall.
She lit the moon.
Snow began to fall.

And she laid the snow
as if at home again,
proudly, under the lights
of Jerusalem.

DANNIE ABSE

Of Two Languages
For Hanoch Bartov

1.

Citizen Dov walking on Mount Carmel
heard Agnon speaking Yiddish to a companion.
"How can you," complained Dov, "a five-star scholar,
a great *Hebrew* author, a Nobel-prize winner,
prophet amongst men, Solomon amongst Kings,
a genuine, first-class somebody (destined for
a State Funeral) how can *you* speak Yiddish?"

"Observe which way we're walking," replied Agnon.
"Downhill. Downhill, I always speak Yiddish.
Uphill—break forth into singing, ye mountains—
uphill, I speak the language of Isaiah."

2.

Dov, you know Hebrew, you also know Yiddish.
Did you not speak to God in Hebrew
when you spoke to men in Yiddish?

All those used-up, ascetic centuries
of studying the evidence of 22 consonants;
the 23rd would not have destroyed the world.

Now in Hebrew, bellicose, you say, "Go away."
Once, softly in Yiddish, you begged, "Leave me alone."

Tell me, what's the word for "mercy" in Hebrew?
In Yiddish, "mercy" must have many synonyms.
Say now in Yiddish: "Exile. Pogrom. Wandering.
Holocaust."
Say now in Hebrew: "Blessed Art Thou O Lord."

SEYMOUR MAYNE

Abraham Sutzkever

Tired and bloodshot
your aging eyes
match your bald
pate and full moustache
memento of your girth
and Partisan strength

You speak and sing
always of some past's
indefinite future
which is not the present
ever but that frozen
waste where unpeopled
the ghosts of millions
wind into the snow
and darkening light—
northern hell
of the world, Siberia
where history
is grimly imminent

Surrounded by paintings
Vilna mementos and nameplates
here in your flat
over lightwashed Tel Aviv—
here you say
you never write
But only find yourself reflected
in the books and portraits

Hurrying you seem
always rushing and writing
poems as all poets now do
in haste, secretly,
unseen in no man's
land, invisible place,
the impossible promised land
where all the refugee words
are gathered and make shelter

ROBERT ESHMAN

Acts of Loving Kindness

On Sunday I found eleven shoes
in Mea She'arim, the kind the black-
coats wear, thin charcoal leather slippers.
I gathered them, then, coming before a
beggar, gave them, not shekels, over.
"Why?" she hissed, spitting at the
trampled, odd-sized *minyan*.
I left, then soon returned, saying nothing but,
"Madam, do you by any chance sell shoes?"
She wiped her hands against her skirt
and asked, "What size?"

LAYLE SILBERT

Belonging

my father belonged first
to his native place
in America he belonged
where he lived
his true being belonged
in Israel even before
it was born
he made speeches
filled with passion & belief

on the streets of Jerusalem
do I see my father again
sniffing the holy air
in a Tel Aviv cafe
confronting the Knesset
& on a stroll in the Old City?

until he died
he was afraid to go
where he belonged the most

JONATHAN MAGONET

Uncomfortable in Jerusalem

For the time being
I'll keep my *kippah* in my pocket
and wear it to study, in *shul*,
and on the streets of Jerusalem,
at least on Shabbat.

I'll tease the "reformers"
to whose curious company I belong
and apologize to the "orthodox"
whose power I admit with unease.

I'll continue to feel a vocation,
dislike services, pray each day,
journey, when the chance arises,
with Christians and Muslims I trust.

I'll try to teach from experience,
learn from any teacher,
see through what is phony,
and sometimes fight.

I'll choose my "religious" friends
for their love, for their whimsy,
and my "secular" ones
for their faith.

For the time being
as a reasonable Jew
and Englishman,
I'll try not to cheat
and remain uncomfortable
in Jerusalem.

RICHARD MICHELSON

Questions for Grandfather

I. The Flight

    We circle. We circle
    until Grandfather's dizzy,
    his head spinning like the glass globe
    on which he'd measure, in inches,
    the distance from America. As he prayed,
    blood would pulse through his veins,
    his forehead mapping the traditional
    borders of Israel. Leaning
    towards the window I can see
    no further than the fear reflected
    in the dark clouds under my eyes.
    I watch a prayer
    dance down my grandfather's throat.
    The clouds dissolve. I think
    I can see Jerusalem.

II. The Walled City

    These catwalks weave
    like so many false messiahs
    through the Walled City.
    The paths turn, reconsider,
    circle back. Beneath the weight
    of an eight-foot plastic cross
    men pose their wives. All along
    the Via Dolorosa, women wave
    as Grandfather walks
    straight towards the Wailing Wall.

III. The Temple Mount

Here, where even stones are symbols,
and to stumble on a tree root
becomes the surest sign; somewhere
near the Holiest of Holies
my eyes turn from the rock
where Abraham kissed Isaac,
and all belief and holy men are left behind.
Here, where Grandfather fears to step,
I walk down the paths his prayers
have carved through history, while he
waits on the side street, where,
like Moses, all old men shake
at the edge of their dreams.

IV. The Mount of Olives

One does not visit the Mount of Olives
to escape the smell of death.
I have many questions
to ask of Grandfather
but he is both silent
and sad. When the messiah calls
these first lucky few to heaven,
he will be burrowing underground
from his grave in New York,
certain that Heaven is
an overbooked flight
with just so many seats.

Maria Olt

On a hillside in Jerusalem
under the hammer sun, she lifts

a little carob tree, the tree of John
the Baptist, and sets it

into its hole. Solid as a house,
she is called Righteous, a Christian

who hid Jews in Hungary. Her hair clings
around her broad face as she bends

with the hoe, carefully heaping the soil
around the roots. She builds a rim of dirt

on the downhill side and pours water from
the heavy bucket. She waits until the earth

sucks the water up, then pours again
with a slow wrist. The workmen

sent to help her, stand aside, helpless.
She straightens up. Her eyes are wet.

Tears come to her easily.
The small Jewish woman she saved

stands beside her, dry-eyed.
Thirty-five years ago, as they watched

the death train pass, faces and hands
silent between the slats, the girl

had cried, I want to go with them!
No, said Maria, you must understand,

if you go, I will go with you.

ELAINE STARKMAN

In the Kibbutz Laundry
for Rivke Cooper

The number on her arm
appears as I rest
in the dead heat
of the noon sun
no longer a nightmare
of story-book horror
that I read in America
twenty years ago

She's lived somehow—God knows
is here now working
in the kibbutz laundry
her hands move in an act of love

When the day ends
and night winds blow
I search out her clear blue eyes
but they reveal nothing

Yet engraved on her arm
lives a page of history
that all the soap
and all the rubbing
can never wash away

Degania Beit, 1969

RICHARD MICHELSON

For Forty Years My Mother

For forty years my mother clipped the wings
of newspapers, stories of men's memories,
unable to fly, rising suddenly like smoke.

In Israel, the gathering of survivors approaches.
Sophisticated new computers are programmed
to bring together families and friends.

For forty years my mother saw, each morning,
her youngest brother alive on street corners,
his number hidden under shirt sleeves or serpent tattoos.

"I remember," she says, as her sisters stretch
across Jerusalem, city of hope. They call out
camp names, last seen, countries of birth. Wait,

they beg their children, a little longer.
But already we are drowning in a red sea of grief,
longing for the dryness of the desert.

THEODORE WEISS

The Here and Now
for Yehuda Amichai

Though you live in a little country,
crammed and crisscrossed with debris,
the past oppressive many times over—
where you buy your grapes, David, pausing,
eyes a fiery dark girl, a lusty song
riding his breath, the old dance urgent
at his body; where you buy your bread
Christ, stumbling, stoops to heavy lumber—
you insist on your own loves and griefs,
on living your own life.
                              So you love
this city, but mainly as it goes on
living its own life, across its roofs
the lines flapping, not gaudy banners,
but sheets and diapers, pants and slips,
as if rehearsing private pleasures.

And though you know you cannot win,
you play the game with all the skill
and love that you can muster, hoping
to keep it, keep it going, whatever
the fierceness in it, while you learn
the repertoire of your opponent's wrist,
the repertoire of your own commands,
with every stroke surprising you,
as in a woman's glance the abundance
glinting of her passion stored away.

Those opposing roles, victor, victim
both, when they require re-enacting,
the moon as ever plays the luminous dome

above your god-and-man-scarred rock,
responsive to each nuance of the light
informing it with this, the latest scene.

The sweat you've shared between you,
juices drying on your hands and moon-
lit belly, swirls out of the rutted, stain-
stiff sheets a fragrance stronger, more
anointing, than the myrrh, the frank-
incense the magi brought, a gleam
that would eclipse their beaten gold.

YEHUDA AMICHAI

When a Man Has Been Away

When a man has been away from his homeland a long time,
his language becomes more and more precise
less and less impure,
like precise clouds of summer
on their blue background
which will never pour down rain.

Thus all those who were once lovers
still speak the language of love, sterile
and clear, never changing, and never
getting any response.

But I, who have stayed here, dirty my mouth
and my lips and my tongue.
In my words there is garbage of soul
and refuse of lust and dust and sweat.
Even the water I drink in this dry land
is urine recycled back to me
through complicated circuits.

Translated from the Hebrew by the author

VI

THE BORDER

FLORENCE ELON

Akbar

Packed in one kibbutz shack
we hear the news in six
languages. Each listens
to his own, then turns
back to the phonograph.
The walls shake, ready to split.

Sick of war news
I walk out, wander on
a snake trail. It winds down . . .

Brown grass turns yellow. Sun
slants westward. Have I crossed
into enemy land? There, ahead:
lush green clusters.

A veiled girl bends,
fills her pail
like Leah or Rachel
and sees me clomp in boots:
a spy, staring at her?

She leads me silently
up steps cut into dirt
past coops that stink of dung
to her own hut—
seams splitting, roof aslant,
just like the one I left.

A young man in khakis
opens the door and shakes my hand,
"Come in." She brews coffee

over an open fire;
he tells me this is Akbar,
Arab, relocated
because of "incidents."
I don't question further.

We sip from one delicate cup.
Bitter mints melt on our tongues.
"Now we are friends,"
he says. "Are you afraid?"

NANCY DATAN

On Ordering Dog Tags

Should the address be engraven, "Jerusalem, Israel"
or just "Jerusalem"? Statesmen have said
that while Israel stands, Jerusalem
will never again be split.
                    Not by the Vatican,
not by the Arabs, not by the vote
in the United Nations: we will hold Jerusalem
while we have breath and blood.

So be it, then: "Jerusalem."
It's cheaper, briefer, and more politic,
and gives a bit of drama to the tags.

O yes: my blood is rising already,
I am waiting to pour it onto the waiting hills.

25 VIII 67

BARBARA D. HOLENDER

The Tank

Kibbutz Gonen, Israel

Two were captured from the Syrians.
No trophies, said the government, seizing one.
The other, hidden under brush,
became a plaything for the children,
first generation to grow up above ground.

Disarmed, disembowelled,
painted in pastel camouflage,
it blended into the garden.

Give back the gun, said the children
not to be pacified with less
than the genuine, but quite content
that it sat harmless as a pied bullfrog
among the blossoms.

The dark magic
that turned children into moles
in subterranean playrooms
could make it bloom again
with fire.

KINERETH GENSLER

The Border

The war broke out in autumn at the empty
border between sweet grapes and oranges.
                                        Yehuda Amichai

War or peace, the border is never empty,
growing its wildflowers and weeds,
making the most of a difficult position.

And the cash crops aren't meant for your table.
You're an old hand dragging that wagon to market:
grapes, oranges, wheat—

whatever the harvest, it's earmarked for export.
You ship it abroad, make do
with dandelion greens and milkweed.

When war breaks out,
weeds will sustain you.
You rely on chicory,
And the Good Soldier Thistle . . .

This story belonged to your mother,
it's the one she loved telling:

> At nightfall, after the first World War, in those months
> of upheaval, stranded in a brokendown car in the hills of
> Judea, afraid of the isolate terrain, afraid of the driver, she
> saw from the road's edge a blue flower, followed it into a
> stony field, and picked it.
> In the fading light it was a beacon, blue as amulets are
> blue. Reaching through thorns, her fingers uncovered a
> box and wires, and a voice came to her out of the ground:
> *What number are you calling? May I help you?*

After a time she answered, forcing herself to speak into a field telephone, left over from the war, still connected. She told what landmarks she had seen, where she had come from and where she was headed.

And rescue came. They lifted the car and driver into a huge lorry, scooping her up, taking her straight to her destination!

From her fear, a woman makes a story
and tells it to her daughters.
Telling it, she names it:
The Blue Thistle.

In the blue blaze of thorn along the border,
in the desolate spaces,
a real voice speaks from the ground,
a weed called by its name becomes a flower.

Something brave is growing.

MYRA SKLAREW

At the Syrian Border

Walking between two mine fields
I pretend I am a tourist here: What trees,
I say. What mountains. I mouth
slogans bitter as a salt sea.

The wind feeds on the basalt rock.
Under every eucalyptus there is
the yawning shadow of a bunker. My people
is an armed camp.

I remember a boy who made a bridge
of his body for the others to climb across.
They turned him into air and fire and earth.
And here is the place where a father

let his child down a knotted sheet
like Jacob, only not going up.
One child by one child down the ladder
of knots and when he himself climbed

down for the last time he found each one
murdered. O Jacob let us put away
our strange gods. My people is an armed
camp. Her sons wear old faces.

CARYL BULMER

Yamit
Sinai Peninsula 1982

a wind from Africa
blows out
our candles in the night—
slow,
the desert's tide
flows in

there is a word
that quivers
like a lowering flag,
yesterday full of water meanings,
        fruits and flowering shade—

        shalom
        we come to sow

there is a word
now dry
stranded in the creep of sand—

        shalom
        we go

that we may know
the deepest meaning
of the word:

peace
O Lord of waters and of loss
let be

Subduing the Nile

The famous picture shows Carter and Sadat
    in an embrace.
A European embrace
Cupped like petals, but not quite
Their fingers open soft as the ribs of
    leaves
As the touch of parents
But it is not a hug, it has more the
    sinew of tree trunks
It is a covenant of arms
A circle of eyes that absorb each other
Each man a father to the other
Each man a son to the other
No one knowing who is who
So that when the semitic wails of mourning
    were heard
It could not be known whether they were
    Hebraic or Arabic
For death runs together
The loudspeakers moan for days through
    the alleys and markets
Under the tents, in the temples and synagogues
Inside any space that poor people especially
    fill.
They grow tight against the ovens that still make
    bricks and clay pots
They grow tight against the trains that still carry
    them to Cairo or the Delta
The way a stream carries insects
An old, straight circle that drives
Their oxen from the same beginnings
Starting or stopping, anywhere along the circle.

ELAINE STARKMAN

Without a Single Answer

Soon I'll leave this heat, this babel of tongue on tongue,
babies cooing, crying all hours of the night and day,
rough kids who'd never touch you when you walk
alone in the dark after Sabbath—leather brown faces,
black ones, European eyes, red Romanian hair—the
Moroccan cleaning woman who calls me "mutik,"
Jacques' chansons in Hebrew and French, bow-legged
grandmothers at the beach, beautiful young German girls,
wearing Stars of David, their eyes full of hope

leave stubbing tarry toes in the warm nurturing sea with
jellyfish, half-eaten corn cobs, Ellen's falcon that
hangs in midair motionless with faith, army helicopters
whirling up mirages of sand, sand always in my
shoes and later in my dreams with all the verbs I never
learned, the fist of sun blazing down on our outings, bus
trips to the Dead Sea, our boat ride across the Kinneret

that locks us together, Arab and Jew—swaying,
moving, dancing sensually to the thrum of *oud* and
drum, molding us toward love that retreats at the other
shore:

> *Don't ask for more than this moment*

Arabs holding hands, smoking hookahs into the night,
three Egyptians among us, brothers who travel here
now, while we Americans tease them in our awful
twang

leave the *midbar*, Massada, stones of Jerusalem, the
Wall, digs, mail strikes, arches, alleyways, assault of
armpits, crying cats, Ellen's pines that sway in minyan,
joyful pilgrims, praying black-robed Jews in the July
heat, this two-star hotel with its boiled chicken, broken
toilets, phones, air-conditioners, and whispered rumors
of a kidnapped soldier

I'll catch two planes traveling from east to west where
I have no need for verbs, amulets, news every hour,
self-tests when history pokes out from the litter
and burrows into my skin, no need for translations
of tempers on buses, in banks, in queues,
in the dining room

and when I return to America if friends quiz me I'll
simply say, I came, I saw, I found no answers.

Ulpan Akiva, 8/1/1987

SEYMOUR MAYNE

Mount Scopus

The silence on the heights—nothing is heard from the neigh-
boring hill. The cries must be wandering in the valleys. The
lost tribes of vows have disappeared among us and once in a
while we recognize them—for a moment—in our chameleon
speech.

SHARON KESSLER

Even Our Trees Fight

Even our trees fight. They plant olive trees,
we pull them out and plant pine trees.
                    Meron Benvenisti

pine
against
olive,
and where olive
is uprooted,
pine digs in, and
in the front lines
our houses,
prefab
against stone,
and our beasts
of burden,
bulldozer
against mule,
whole towns pitted
against villages,
even the streetlamps
flying in a rage
against grape arbors,
and the stone terraces
advancing
down the hillside
row by row.

And our children,
who might just as well
live together, hate with the hatred

of olive
for pine,
hate with the stupidity
of the bulldozer
and the mule,
while on both sides
hills and valleys
surrender
conquered by olive,
occupied by pine,
and the stones
wrench themselves up
from the extraordinary landscape,
helter-skelter, free at last.

VII

WE WATCH THE RAIN
AND SPEAK OF PEACE

Yehuda Amichai

From "Laments on the War Dead"

Is all this sorrow? I don't know,
I stood in the cemetery dressed
in the camouflage clothing of a live man, brown
pants and a shirt yellow as the sun.

Graveyards are cheap and unassuming.
Even the wastebaskets are too small to hold
the thin paper that wrapped the store-bought flowers.
Graveyards are disciplined, mannered things.
"I'll never forget you," reads
a small brick tablet in French,
I don't know who it is who won't forget
who's more unknown than the one who's dead.

Is all this sorrow? I think
so. "Be consoled in building the land." How
long can we build the land,
to gain in the terrible, three-sided
game of building, consolation, and death?
Yes, all this is sorrow. But
leave a little love always lit,
like the nightlight in a sleeping infant's room,
not that he knows what light is
and where it comes from, but it gives him
a bit of security and some silent love.

Translated from the Hebrew by
Warren Bargad and Stanley F. Chyet

CAROL GREENBERG

We Watch the Rain and Speak of Peace

I am old,
you are young;
You remind me that when we came to this place,
we lifted the veil of dust from the face of the land
to find dark brown soil, rich loam waiting.
We laughed at the long legged white storks
snatching worms in our red tractor's wake.
You finger the scar on your chest
ask me for a second time:
      What price peace?
The smell of earth and rain intoxicates.

We are ready to leave as we came.
We have not much to take.
Six o'clock.
You take the gun from the corner,
pull on your black boots.
I know you will milk the cows,
trample the new young shoots, so new
the soil is still fresh under your nails,
you tell me that one of the cows will probably calf.

Tonight our nerves are bad.
We will make small talk;
there is a new moon.
The rain has passed unheard.
Passover is tomorrow.
You stand in the open door
your hand on your gun.
You speak of peace again. We watch the rain.
You put your hand to my hand.
Together we watch a falling star.

ZELDA

Pause

for the terrorist who saved an Israeli prisoner from the hands
of the other terrorists who wanted to torture him

A gesture of the hand
wipes out the fantasies of torture—
a gesture
by one of the wolves of suicide,
an eager youth who suddenly
set hate aside
because his soul revealed to him:
hatred lies,
hatred lies,
hatred lies.
And the force of his imaginings
burst upon a new path
with the sounds of childhood
and of miracles.
When the primordial good
awoke in him,
he saved the prisoner.
When a river flowed from his inner Eden,
he gave him water
to revive him in the desert.
Slowly the monster of vengeance
retreated,
and fresh worlds of hope
and the joy of wells rich with water
were revealed.
Oh! Both of them knew—
this was not the whole truth,
this was a pause

on a green island,
the island beyond all nations,
beyond all outlets.

On this island, in one of the caves,
peace opened its eyes.

Translated from the Hebrew by Marcia Falk

IRENA KLEPFISZ

East Jerusalem, 1987: Bet Shalom

To a Palestinian woman whom I am afraid to name

Whether we like it or not
we must sit here. What we feel
does not matter. We are the heirs
our legacy is in the air we breathe
the ground we stand on.

One of us lives in the neighborhood
you were raised in
where you took   your first steps
and met the world.
Then everyone left.
Your uncles and aunts
carried their belongings
and left. It was '48.

You ask us:

> *Do you understand   can you imagine*
> *what it must feel like to me?*
> *to all of us?*
> *I do not go back to those neighborhoods.*
> *I just don't feel right.*
> *Do you understand*
> *what it means to all of us?*

We understand   we remember history
and understand it all:
the need for safety   a safety
no one else can take away.
The need for control
not waiting on line   to get attention
or for the consciences of others   to awaken.

We understand what it means to have children
who die   children who live and learn to be proud
of who they are.

Doubts break through.
This is in the air   the reluctance
to have understanding be enough.
We ask: didn't you omit
part of the picture
didn't you leave out a piece   along the border
a piece of sky   the very peak of a mountain
the bus bombed   the children in the schoolhouse
peaceful farmers   ploughing fields—
you left out part of the picture.

Understanding wraps us again   tightly
towards each other.
We remember the camps: during   and after.
During: there was murder   and resistance
more murder   *and after*:   there was determination
sneaking in at night   no lights burning
the small boats   the landings on the beach
when everyone else had said: don't go there
or there or there   or who wants them anyway
they've always been trouble   *and again after*:
bombings   massacres
we understand the actions of a desperate people.

Doubts break us apart
We can barely breathe. We ask:

Why are you our problem too? We can hardly hold
our own. Why can't you just blend in
with your own kind?

Whether we like it   or not
we must sit here   and this is in the air.
You say to us:
>   *You must understand*
>   *how it is for me.*
>   *You are writers*
>   *Write about it.*
You mean: Our voices carry.
Yours alone does not.

All of us part. You move off   in a separate
direction. The rest of us return
to the other Jerusalem. It is night.
I still hear your voice. It is in the air
now   with everything else   except sharper
clearer. I think of your relatives
your uncles and aunts   I see the familiar
battered suitcases   cartons with strings
stuffed pillowcases
children sitting on people's shoulders
children running to keep up

Always   there is migration
on this restless planet   everywhere
there is displacement   somewhere
someone is always telling   someone else
to move on   to go elsewhere.

Night.   Jerusalem.   *Yerushalayim.*
Jerusalem.   If I forget thee
Oh Jerusalem   Jerusalem   Hebron
Ramallah   Nablus   Qattana   if I
forget thee oh Jerusalem
Oh Hebron   may I forget
my own past   my pain
the depth of my sorrows.

AVITAL TALMOR

Historical Boomerang

What did they think, the old dreamers,
fled here on their burning passions
(stoked by two millennia of pining souls
and that apocalyptic test
humanity had not cared enough to pass)
to build Jerusalem anew (Amen)—
that we'd swallow whole the bait
of sacrifice and glory
they force-fed us on
so we'd follow up and emulate
where they left off?

Now as they see
their lofty dream of a country
zealously bequeathed to us
take on our image
they scream in indignation
that we've let them down.

For all their wisdom
and commendable achievements,
they didn't take into account
that too much history emasculates.

SEYMOUR MAYNE

The Abrupt Siren of Beit Hakerem

The abrupt siren of Beit Hakerem
must be fixed, people.
It stabs out at the least likely
moment, shears into our hearing
then dies down as suddenly
as a fish, bait in mouth
and torn of tongue, dives back
for the safer depths.

Where does that cold-blooding call
hide its shark-eyed nose?
Whoever plays with this leviathan:
beware, this is no goldfish.
It waits for the darkest storm
to come tearing at our breasts,
its bolt of a body bursting forward
like the horned javelin of Gabriel
or the last angels
who do not spare even
the zigzag of a hesitating nod
as they signal for the wail
and pouring of fire.

ALICIA OSTRIKER

The Bride

i.

Jerusalem sits on her mountains, a woman
Who knits and frowns, going over and over her story,
Sifting it, every detail memorized, magnified,
Interpreted. How many lovers, what caresses, what golden
Fornications, what children of brilliant intellect
Sucking hard at her nipples,
What warriors, what artists.

There was a time for riches, a time for poverty.
She has gone begging in the streets, yes,
And she has danced in her rags.

And today they are killing for her
Among the stones. What woman would not
Be thoroughly proud. They love her, they love her
Above the queens
Of the earth, above the other beauties.

ii.

The cats in Jerusalem form the secret
Government. They are sisters. They have hearts
As black as eels, or hearts as red
And wise as pomegranates.

They insinuate everywhere, everywhere.
Under the shady orange trees
Sit three or four,
By the ruined wall a score,

Nine surround the Dome of the Rock.
Six yawn, their mouths open as orchids,
Revealing needle teeth.

So forget the rabbis and their frozen Law,
A rod that likes
Hitting a child's fingers, and making
That satisfying sting of punishment.
Forget about the members
Of Parliament, shouting yet reasonable
Like jewelry merchants counting on your goodwill.
Forget the competitive brands of Christians
Selling postcards of sexy crucifixions
Who peer from shadowy galleries of the Church
Of the Holy Sepulchre, the livid saints
And martyrs dissolving into grimy mosaic darkness.
Forget the revolutionary students.
Cheap thrills, cheap thrills.
Forget even the fleshy mothers
Sarah and Hagar,
Praying, shopping, cooking,
Complaining. Forget their apartments, their leaky
Sinks, and the shortened screams when the bad news comes
On the evening radio about their sons
Who were tall and handsome, who were a little careless
In Hebron, or the Golan, or Beirut.

Forget the mayor, his rosy stitching and patching.
Forget making the world a better place.

Blood and sand.
What is reality and what is fiction?
The cats crouch, the cats
Have a saying: You've seen one corpse,
You've seen them all. The black, the white, the gray,

Stealthy, overt and sleek,
The runners, the striped ones,
The ones that look like apricots and milk,
Are receiving orders from a small, blackened
Bronze Egyptian cat
In the Rockefeller Museum,
The cat of dire memory, whose heart,
The size of an olive, is heavier
Than an iron cannonball.

Heavy because so angry,
So angry.

SHIRLEY KAUFMAN

Meeting in Ramallah

We get down on the floor at first
because the kittens are there
and it's easy to play with them.
Fierce little faces. Sakhar
shows me her favorite,
lifting its chin.

Where can it lead? From her home
in this Arab city, her taut friends
over the teacups. The color
of license plates tells us
who we are.

I might have stayed
on my own side where it's common
to say the wrong things
and be forgiven.

It's not just a matter of truth
or occupation.
We each have our fables,
the sweet cakes
stick to our fingers as we speak.

The kittens roll over
and the mother finds them,
nursing one hunger at a time.

As it gets late
we can't depend on the stars.

If I tell you
today's the Sabbath
then it's Saturday unless it's Friday
and it's your turn to sleep
late in the morning or to pray,
unless it's Sunday and the bells are ringing.

If you tell me
the soul is a lame dog
thrashing its tail, one ear
for the world's contagions, one
for the master with his own versions,

and if we tug at this city
in our blindfolds
until it splits and goes
sailing over the mountains,

what will become of your fast days
and my atonement, what
will become of us?

Prologue to a Poem

This poem is a poem about people:
What they think and what they want
And what they think they want
Besides this there's not much in the world
We ought to care about. And it's a poem about human deeds,
Because the deeds are more important
Than the things that aren't done. And every man wants
His deeds to be remembered long after the things
Left undone are forgotten.
And it's also a poem about a grand and spacious land
And when the darkness descends, wrapped in sunset
Like pity, a man might
Mistake it for a desert and so it's obviously also a poem
About a desert and about human beings crossing hot sand which moves
In their blood and it's a poem about people everywhere: How
They feel when the blue night sings the song of caravans
And how they taste sand in the charred fuselage which falls and sings
Like a burning love note: Instead of prose, this is a poem
About houses torn down and others put up in their place
But different from those which came before: Poets will sing
Of houses as long as there are poets in the world, but maybe
Not as long as there are houses. And finally, these are poems
About war and were written in the heat of battle and at a writing desk
  and without hope.

Translated from the Hebrew by
Warren Bargad and Stanley F. Chyet

MICHAEL CASTRO

Hear O Israel, O Palestine

Not even the desert sun
can slake this sorrow.
Not even the desert sands
can bury the dead.

Cain & Abel are eternal.
No matter what you call this space
it's still a desert.

Yet all the prophets agree:
God is One. Man in His image.
We cannot escape
who we are. But where
are the prophets that can make us see
our own reflection
in the mirror of stone?
The mirror shattered by stones.
Our own Godless images
fragmented,
invoking the Name profanely
confused. Blood seeps
into these sands, quickening
them so we can sink,
shouting at each other as we disappear
into our dream of security.
Or revenge.

The sun bakes our fevered brows
& the blood rushes
to our heads.
Europe is everywhere.
Holy Wars.

Our minds swim
in the dry air.

*   *   *

Pray for this desert place—
For those who return home.
For memories that turn to raindrops.
Pray to the empty cave of the prophet,
to the Palaces of Silence.

Pray quietly, for what does exist & therefore can
flourish:
     the clarity of air
     we all can breathe;
     the miracle
     of trees;
     the light
     in human eyes.

LEAH SCHWEITZER

A Rally for Peace

that day   the park   rolling slopes
green-cut grass   bodies soothed by sun
intifada   a new word   to try
on the tongue   we wait   for the
Peace Now rally   to begin   young
& old   here   to try to make sense
of shattering news   from the West Bank
        from Gaza

that day   the park   the singing
in harmony   "Hinei matov umanayim . . ."
"Ya aseh shalom . . ."   then with
no warning   we're surrounded
by protestors   a bad dream
but we're awake   they
worm their way through   to disrupt
harass   as the speakers   struggle
to be heard   over catcalls
& accusations: "Traitors!"
        "Nazis!"   "Murderers!"

a boy   twelve or thirteen
blasts obscenities through a megaphone
someone asks, "Young man, would you stop
long enough to listen   to what's
being said?"   "No way!" he bellows
& beams   at his father   for signs
        of approval

curses   fly like bullets   Yael Dayan
olive face   long straight hair
thick husky voice   urges:

"We can't be occupiers   and be
democratic   at the same time!"
the park   is engulfed   in shouting
        & screaming: "Nazis!"   "Murderers!"

to our right   hecklers   in their
twenties   savor   the pandemonium
smile broad smiles   of amusement
when Betty Friedan stands to speak
one of them howls, "Bella? Is it Bella?
Go home, Bella, to your women's movement—
leave Israel to us!"   Friedan delivers
her speech   but her voice   is lost
        in the din

a six-year-old   sobs   clings
to his father's pant-legs   confusion
crimps his rosy face   he & I
the two of us   frightened
my thoughts   fly across the world:
a Palestinian six-year-old   clings
to *his* father's legs   and now
three of us are frightened
many of us are frightened
that day   the park
        the tension

there   in the epicenter
the eye of a storm just beginning
that day   the park   a rally
        for peace

13 March 1988
Roxbury Park, Los Angeles

VIII
HOW BEAUTIFUL
ARE THY TENTS

Yehuda Amichai

My Mother Died on Shavuot

My mother died on Shavuot when they finished counting the Omer,[*]
her oldest brother died in 1916, fallen in the war,
I almost fell in 1948,
and my mother died in 1983.
Everyone dies at some counting,
long or short,
everyone falls in a war,
they all deserve a wreath and a ceremony and an official letter.
When I stand by my mother's grave
it's like saluting
and the hard words of the Kaddish a salvo
into the clear summer skies.

We buried her in Sanhedria next to my father's grave,
we kept the place for her
as in a bus or a cinema:
Leaving flowers and stones so no one would take her place.

(Twenty years ago this graveyard was
on the border, facing the enemy's positions.
The tombstones were a good defense against the tanks.)

But in my childhood there was a botanical garden here.
Lots of flowers with frail wooden tags
bearing names of flowers in Hebrew and Latin:
Common Rose, Mediterranean Sage,
Common Scream, Tufted Weeping,

---

*Sheaf of corn; 49 days between the second day of Passover and Shavuot
(Pentecost).

Annual Weeping, Perennial Mourning,
Red Forget-Me-Not, Fragrant Forget-Me-Not,
Forget-me-not, forget.

Translated from the Hebrew by Barbara and Benjamin Harshav

Desecration of the Sabbath

On the Sabbath my dead husband comes to take me to the memorial service for his soul, a service to be held in the synagogue. I don't have a car, and there are no busses running today, nor do I have money for a taxi. The thorns at the roadside do not sway to any breeze, the bathers at the sea are surprised to see the black flag atop the lifeguard's booth and don't return to shore, and we drive and drive. He says nothing. Pale and thin, he's come from the land of the dead. We keep on driving. The synagogue where his parents pray is far away, thus we travel by car, thus we cross the boundary of the Sabbath, we desecrate the Sabbath. What cancels what? To go through with the memorial service, or honor the Sabbath by resting? But what rest can there be on the Sabbath when the wars are at each of the One Hundred Gates,[*] and we can't get to the sea.

Don't worry, he says to me. The Yeshiva boys prayed at the Cave of Machpelah on the Sabbath, while I worked on the Sabbath for the sake of my people. The Yeshiva boys live, while I and Zvika and Ofer are dead, and you are afraid of desecrating the Sabbath. Interpreters of the law arise in every generation. Perhaps the nation has been redeemed, but we have no rabbi and no redeemer.

Translated from the Hebrew by Sharon Kessler

*Mea She'arim, One Hundred Gates, an ultraorthodox neighborhood in Jerusalem.

Rivka Miriam

Fastening the Light of the Sabbath Candles

Fastening the light of the Sabbath candles
to my eyes, my palms are tents
where my fathers rested in the desert.
The light wraps itself to my eyes.
The light gathers into me.
When they wandered in the desert
the openings of their tents
were turned one from the other.
While they wandered in the desert their openings
covered clouds. Sand and light mixed.
My fingers are brittle.
My hair is veiled.

Translated from the Hebrew by Linda Zisquit

HAMUTAL BAR-YOSEF

Cry, Sheep

Cry, sheep,
thick-headed in darkness. Cry,
sheep. You spoiled the Sabbath.
In the industrial area the sand lies clean,
enlightened, sparkling with gold buttons, changing
into a beige suit with pockets.
And to whom and what for?
A sheep locked in a carpentry shop
licking the rolled sawdust, going crazy,
sick for water.
Yea though she walk
through the whole carpentry shop
there isn't a soul in the industrial area
no living voice except her,
spoiling the Sabbath
with bleats full of sawdust.

Translated from the Hebrew by Yishai Tobin

LEORA BAUMGARTEN

The Land and I

Numbers: XX

We cling together
like children
afraid of thunder.

I came
like the goat
my father bought
for two zuzim
to this land
of confounded blessings
only to encounter
talking mules.

E. M. SOLOWEY

The Woman and the Sound of the Wind

The wind used to whimper
By the rock walls of the valley
Strike at the corners
Of the bare square houses
Move the white sand
From dune to dune
Like lonely smoke

Today the wind swoops
Down the green aisles
Of the date palms
Flings up a glowing haze
Of dust
From the citrus blossoms
Hums in the alfalfa
And the silvery oats
Stroke my children's hair
As they sweat in the sunlight

EDMUND PENNANT

Storks

My stance of prayer: flight,
easily misunderstood for modesty;

others, more at ease, hurdle
the eighteen benedictions, with time
to gaze at a strange wheeling of storks
high above the holiest of walls.

The sky's alive with them.
They are pausing en route
to Syria, to contemplate
the Jews, so rich

in immanence of miracle:
sunfire seen piercing
the pale tertiaries, prayer-
shawls rimmed with flame;

but the birds
are not consumed.

YEHUDA AMICHAI

How Beautiful Are Thy Tents

How beautiful are thy tents, Jacob.
Even now, when there are neither tents nor Jacob's
tribes, I say, how beautiful.

Oh, may there come something of redemption,
an old song, a white letter,
a face in the crowd, a door opening
for the eye, multicolored
ice cream for the throat,
oil for the guts, a warm
memory for the breast.

Then my mouth will open wide
in everlasting praise,
open like the belly of a
wide-open calf hung on a hook
in a butcher's shop of the Old City market.

Translated from the Hebrew by the author

RUTH FAINLIGHT

The Mount of Olives

Eternity has staked its claim
to the hills around Jerusalem.
The dead have prime territory,
every slope a cemetery,
caves, crypts, and sepulchres,
catacombs hollowed out like ovens
under olive groves and churches.

Cars and buses grind their way
below the Wall and up the valley.
Today, you are the only ones
who want to have the door into
the Sanctuary of Ascension
opened, the boy there tells us. How
can I make a living without tourists?

Sitting on a rock beside
the Tomb of the Prophets, two men,
deaf and dumb, talk with their hands.
If across the Kidron Brook
the Golden Gate unlocked to let
Messiah through and the resurrected
sang His praises, would they notice?

But still the dead ones sleep like babies
undisturbed by bombs, while above them—
rosy as cooks, stern as Crusaders,
pale as Hassids, watchful as soldiers,
silent as angels—spirits hover,
and Eternity settles deeper into
the land around Jerusalem.

Julia Vinograd

The Calling of Jerusalem

"Jerusalem," the Lord called softly
and his voice reached all over the world
till drunkards shook their muddled heads
and the smiles of businessmen wavered briefly,
and lovers were suddenly jealous for a moment,
though not of each other.
But there was no answer.
"Jerusalem," the Lord commanded with all the authority of grief,
"Where are you hiding and why?"

There was no spoken answer
but the air between his hands shrugged of its own accord
and invisible hair, most sacred and desolate, fell against his face.
The Lord carried Jerusalem as a woman carries an unborn child.
"What are you doing here?" he asked her.
"I'm tired," Jerusalem drowsed, but forced herself back into words.
"They look, they pray, they dance, they're exalted,
and then they worry if their parking meters have expired.
I don't mind the wars, I never did, blood has a beautiful color
and my lips are even more beautiful.
But they fight out of habit now, the way they live,
and it's all small and unworthy
and most wearisome.
I'm tired of them, they're not real, they can't see me
and they make me lonely.
I want to stay with you."

"No," said the Lord, "not yet."
"Soon?" pleaded Jerusalem.
"And you promised you'd never ask that,"
the Lord reminded her gently.
"It hurts," she answered simply,

"to be always open in a hive of souls
shut in elegant boxes, but firmly shut.
They don't know how to touch or even how
to want such knowledge.
They don't want me, only my scalp.
They want to win their arguments,
not understand what they're arguing about,
they couldn't care less.
What have I to do with them?"

"You are them," the Lord told her.
"When you were passionate and fickle, so were they.
When you were restless and bitter, so were they.
Now that you want more, they may too.
Go back where you belong and make their parking meters explode;
you've been called a thief many times, pry open those boxes.
Do you think it will happen of itself?"

Jerusalem cast down her eyes,
shuddered as if with cold and nodded.
"But why did you call me then?"
she asked as she re-inhabited her stones.
The Lord caressed the air between his hands,
where she had been.

   "I was lonely," the Lord admitted to nobody,
   "but it's over now."

JAY SHIR

Safad Into Night

God
is great   *akbar*
his sun bows
and his mist   draws Mt. Meron
into sleep open-eyed   with Sirius
and Betelgeuse
and Vega over the hulky prow of big hill

hens fussle   in the fig tree
ma'ariv rises mild as dry hickory smoke
from an autumn
from the shul

a cow lows   out of her
grass-Sabbath
her dewy hooves in bracken
and anemones and golden thistles
crocuses of the dark
press the earth down   toward the earth

no *muezzin* stops singing
His greatness   in quiet
and the great watching
through the dark   which is rest   rest
which is light

YEHUDA AMICHAI

I Have Filtered Out

I have filtered out of the Book of Esther the residue
of vulgar joy, and out of the Book of Jeremiah
the howl of pain in the guts. And out of the
Song of Songs the endless search for love,
and out of the Book of Genesis the dreams
and Cain, and out of Ecclesiastes
the despair and out of the Book of Job—Job.
And from what was left over I pasted for myself a new Bible.
Now I live censored and pasted and limited and in peace.

A woman asked me last night in the darkened street
about the well-being of another woman
who had died before her time, and not in anyone's time.
Out of great tiredness I answered her:
She's fine, she's fine.

Translated from the Hebrew by the author

STANLEY F. CHYET

Sukkot in Jerusalem 5743

eternal cycle of fig and aloe olive and oleander:
a quiet place to watch
the reaching skyward
the kicking free of this unquiet dust
the finding eyes above and a mouth

everything old here
everything left for dead
maneuvers into sunlight

October 1982

IX

ALIVE

Turning

1.

Deadstillness over droughtlands.
Parched, the heart of the matter.
Panic among smaller animals
used to licking water from cool stones.
Over the great farms, a burning-glass
one-eyed and wild as a jack,
the corn snatched in a single afternoon
of the one-eyed jack's impassive stare.

And in that other country
of choices made by others
that country I never chose
that country of terrible leavings and returnings
in that country whose map I carry on my palm
the forests are on fire: history is on fire.

My foot drags in the foothills of two lands;
At the turn the spirit pauses
and faces the high passes:
bloodred granite, sandstone steeped in blood.
At the turn the spirit turns,
looks back—if any follow—
squints ahead—if any lead—
What would you bring along on a trek like this?
What is bringing you along?

2.

In a time of broken hands
in a broken-promised land
something happens to the right hand

Remembering a city, it forgets
flexion, gestures that danced like flames
the lifeline buried in the fist

forgets the pedlar's trinket, fine to finger and lay forth,
the scalpel's path, the tracing of the pulse
the sprinkle of salt and rip of chicken feathers

forgets the wrist's light swivel breaking bread
the matzoh crumb
fingered to secret lips in stinking fog

forgets its own ache, lying
work-stiffened, mute
on the day most like Paradise

Becomes the handle of a club
an enemy of hands
emptied of all memories but one

When the right hand forgets its cunning, what of the other?
Shall we invent its story?
Has it simply lain in trance

disowned, written-off, unemployed?
Does it twitch now, finger and thumb,
does the prickle of memory race through?

When the right hand becomes the enemy of hands
what does the left hand make of their old collaboration?
Pick up the book, the pinch of salt, the matzoh crumb,

hand, and begin to teach.

3.

Finally, we will make change. This eyeflash,
this touch, handling the drenched flyers,
these glances back at history—

riverside where harps hang from the trees,
cracked riverbed with grounded hulks,
unhealed water to cross—

leaving superstition behind—
first our own, then others'—
that barrier, that stream

where swimming against the current will become
no metaphor: this is how you land, unpurified,
winded, shivering, on the further shore

where there are only new kinds of tasks, and old:
writing with others that open letter or brief
that might—if only—we know it happens:

no sudden revelation but the slow
turn of consciousness, while every day
climbs on the back of the days before:

no new day, only a list of days,
no task you expect to see finished, but
you can't hold back from the task.

4.

A public meeting. I glance at a woman's face:
strong lines and soft, listening, a little on guard:
we have come separately, are sitting apart,
know each other in the room, have slept twelve years
in the same bed, attend now to the speaker.

Her subject is occupation, a promised land,
displacement, deracination, two peoples called Semites,
humiliation, force, women trying to speak with women,
the subject is how to break a mold of discourse,
how little by little minds change
but that they do change. We two have fought
our own battles side by side, at dawn, over supper,
our changes of mind have come
with the stir of hairs, the sound of a cracked phrase:
we have depended on something.
What then? Sex isn't enough, merely to trust
each other's inarticulate sounds,
—what then? call it mutual recognition.

5.

Whatever you are that has tracked us this far,
I never thought you were on our side,
I only thought you did not judge us.

Yet as a cell might hallucinate
the eye—intent, impassioned—
behind the lens of the microscope

so I have thought of you,
whatever you are—a mindfulness—
whatever you are: the place beyond all places,

beyond boundaries, green lines,
wire-netted walls
the place beyond documents.

Unnameable by choice.
So why am I out here, trying
to read your name in the illegible air?

—vowel washed from a stone,
solitude of no absence,
forbidden face-to-face

—trying to hand these wraiths
of syllables, breath
without echo, why?

1988

NITZA AGAM

Remaining Anonymous

A quiet morning;
I ride the bus with joggers, church-goers,
teenagers discussing Christ for the Sunday School exam.

San Francisco wakes up, goes to church, and
I love this familiar ritual of riding the bus
on early Sunday mornings.
It is my time to be anonymous.

Now in the restaurant
a dark-haired woman sits next to me.
Her laugh reverberates throughout the place.
She looks Mid-Eastern: long nose, dark hair,
dark skin, shiny eyes.

She smiles; our eyes meet.
She tells me that the space between my teeth
is a sign of good luck. She tells me she is 38,
mother of three grown children, wife to
a much older man. Her name is Emily.
We toast the ten-year difference between us.

I ask her where she's from. I know her answer.
From Ramallah outside Jerusalem.
I'm also from Jerusalem—the Israeli sector.

I tell her about my lover. How he was killed
in the war, his lungs shattered like the glass of a car.
Emily cries, deep heaving sobs, her head on the table.
I comfort her, a hesitating hand on her arm.

She looks up with determination.
"I will not shut up, I will do something for peace,
I will, I will. I can see him, your lover's face,
his eyes, I can see him. You were privileged."
How did she know, how could she see him?
But I believed she did. Was that our bond?

We walk out, not sure we'll meet again,
exchange phone numbers, embrace.
I get back on the bus.
It's not easy to remain anonymous.

Dahlia Ravikovitch

War's End

He came at midnight, his legs cut off,
But his old wounds had long since grown new skin,
He came by the third-floor window
How wondrous it was the way he came in,
We'd had a terrible time of sorrow
And many had lost their dear ones
In streets sown with scraps of paper
Pranced the orphans of the few survivors.

I was frozen as crystal when he came,
And he melted me like wax,
And he transfigured me as the fabric of night
Transfigures the feather of dawn.
His valor was transparent as vapor
Streaming from morning clouds.

Translated from the Hebrew by
Warren Bargad and Stanley F. Chyet

LINDA ZISQUIT

Alive

In this country
if I were to love another man,
pursue him like a lion
till he fell, or spike him
with roses and cloves,
I would remember tomorrow,
my husband off to battle,
my children caught in the cross-fire.

In this country
I cannot pretend innocence.
Even the no man's land,
or the poppy-covered desert
where I sat aching to brush
another man's flesh with a leaf
knows landmarks, signs.

This country wears so many colors
all white and sand and shadowless,
I would travel mindless
as a river
and wash myself free of pardon.
He will return scarred.
I must carry the weapons of a natural life
multiplied, full of rust, inside.

Poem About Men

i.

Alex cannot cry. He envies
My tears. He takes me to his mother's home
Where the piano stands,

A memorial to his father—
A tall man who never recovered
From starvation in the war.

Short, strong Alex winks and laughs
And knows enough to say
He can never come

Close to any woman
For more than two days

ii.

Ronnie looks like a guttersnipe.
He lies and cheats,
And breaks his teeth on American songs

By famous men. He has never done
Anything so serious in his life as
Travel with his dog.

He is dying of leukemia,
Unless he's lying.

iii.

Ariel says he wants
To love me because
I deserve it.

He tells me to clean his flat,
Then takes me to a party where he
Dances with his army buddies.

He takes me to the house of his best friend,
Who lives on
Only in the memories of his strong mother,

His broken sister,
His one-eyed brother.

iv.

In this place, men
Become men in their uniforms,
Scarred and impotent.

They learn to be hard.
They learn to break a woman
In two hours or two weeks.

One beautiful man confides,
"Never trust a man.
Men are all liars."

The truthful men are pious, like
That young one on the bus. When I brushed past,
He drew back as if he'd touched a corpse.

Across the empty causeway, beneath their honest hats,
Eight boys shouted at me five times
The foulest words of love.

MERLE BACHMAN

Even Through the Stone

At night in Jerusalem,
after Shabbat has vanished
in a swirl of oily
smoke and the ash of a candlewick
wet in wine; the spicebox
back on the shelf
Fires can be lit, the ash
can grow long on the ends of cigarettes
break and pile into the ashtrays
while men move through the Talmud,
and a gray light limps from tree
to tree   from page to page

People talk;
the cafes can open their doors
and people talk, all night
about what they hate and
what they love:
war   hashish   rain
the possibilities—

I sit facing a man,
trying to open myself, trying to keep one
moment cupped between us, to see him and not
his history, felt
even through the stone
of this Arab house, that I know the Arabs fled
two wars ago
our whole history
left on the hills around us
chanted in rooms
pacing outside in the streets

In the courtyard of the mosque,
tongues of huge flowers wet the air
with their still tips—
red flowers, opening
for air that dries on the stones like bread
on the wall of an oven   I open my mouth—

The thin, dark men
follow me with their eyes,
picking open figs,
removing the skins   someone brushes past me—
a woman, her face rising
through black veils,
more intense

like a face close to mine in darkness

ESTELLE LEONTIEF

Leaves and Sand

This quiet fall
when gold leaves cling
to oak trees,
I walk under
the wide blue sky
thinking how little I've done;
and that I've made love,
wastefully,
to clean blond northern gods
right out of books.

Now, after a whole life,
I dream of short poets
with darkest hair
and inkstained fingers;
in my mind
a whole land
of dry gold sand
and fertilizing rain.

ABBA KOVNER

Sun-Watchers

Eat and drink
Eat   and drink because
tomorrow we're not going to die   because
we're going to live   because
we're going to go through the whole twilit city
from end to end
that Hebrew city between the veiled hills because
you stand revealed
with me by your side,
my beautiful bridegroom:
we sun-watchers lie down in the   field
we'll be. And until the sun shines
on the wall again we'll lie down again mouth   to mouth
and anyone who's seen it all and said nothing
will see   again
under the tree's spreading boughs
how life is torn
you and I and the canopies overhead
are seven,
my beautiful bridegroom.

Translated from the Hebrew by
Warren Bargad and Stanley F. Chyet

STEVE ROOD

Anna Ticho
Two Small Drawings

I.

Pale hills
tilled to their limit.
Wiry roasted
grasses. Saints
named after
springs. White
spirit smoking
from a cleft.

II.

Two wild
knotted pear
trees twist
from the rubble.
An old couple
blossoming.
It is dangerous.
They cannot hide.

SHARONA BEN-TOV

Clouds over Jerusalem, in Winter

As if they were trying to build on a different thought
the clouds accumulate between sun and the city,
so the beams go wide and break into sheaves of light.
It is as if the clouds were trying to reflect the city

without interference of what makes objects and colors
hard and sharp. From the washed, pale stone they are the breath
between our words, and the soul of Shiloah running underground
released to the upper air, so soft, so limitless.

They are like the explosion between a woman and her lover,
spears, fountains, pregnancies of air, sleep's furrows,
changing without changing their nature,
and one bedsheet rumpling on a line is like a child to them.

They are the builders who would take us up in their arms,
but they have built only a Jerusalem of thoughts.
From the sides of the clouds bloom our epic episodes.
Bloodless. Bloodless.

About the Editors

ELAINE STARKMAN is a Northern California writer, poet, and teacher who lives in Walnut Creek. Her work appears in such anthologies as *The Woman Who Lost Her Names: Selected Writings of American Jewish Women*, Harper & Row, 1980, and *Family: Views from the Interior*, Grey Wolf Press, 1987. In 1987 she co-edited *State of Peace: The Women Speak*, Gull Books, New York, and was a prize winner in the Jessamyn West Annual Fiction Award. Her forthcoming work will appear in *Shaking Eve's Tree*, Jewish Publication Society, 1990, and *Vital Lines*, St. Martin's Press, 1990. Presently she teaches English at Diablo Valley College and Short Story Writing at the University of California, Berkeley Extension. Her experiences in Israel after the Six Day War in 1967 were the impetus for this collection.

LEAH SCHWEITZER is a Los Angeles writer and poet who teaches creative writing and subjects related to the Jewish experience. She studied with the writer Anaïs Nin. Her work appears in *Israel Today*, *Judaica Book News*, *Voices Israel*, *The Jewish Ledger*, *The Literary Monitor*, *Crosscurrents*, *Bitterroot*, *Shirim*, *Confrontation*, the *Small Press Review*, *Apalachee Quarterly* and the *California State Poetry Quarterly*. She translated *In Amerika*, a Yiddish novella written by her grandfather, Chaim Avrom Yachnuk, and published in Poland (1894). In 1986 she was a winner in the Alice Jackson Poetry Prize Competition. She has been on the staff of the Department of Continuing Education at the University of Judaism.

About the Artist

ANTHONY DUBOVSKY studied at the Colegio Nacional de La Plata in Argentina, Reed College in Oregon, the Uniwersytet Warszawski in Poland, and the University of California, at Berkeley. Exhibitions of his work include shows at the Galeria Foksal, Warsaw; The Oakland Museum; Light Gallery, New York; the Magnes Museum, Berkeley; and the Hayden Gallery at MIT. Dubovsky recently received the first annual Max and Sophie Adler Award for his paintings and drawings on Jewish themes, the subject of a major exhibition at the Jewish Community Museum in San Francisco. He lives in Berkeley, where he is an Associate Professor in Visual Studies at the University of California.

The gouache drawings reproduced in this volume are from *Israel*, one of a set of Dubovsky's books published by Alef-Beis. Cover painting: "And See the Land," 1981–82, oil on canvas, 10 × 16 inches.

Contributors

DANNIE ABSE, one of Britain's most distinguished poets, was born in Cardiff in 1923. He is also a playwright, physician, and novelist who blends Celtic, English, and Jewish elements into his writing.

NITZA AGAM, born in 1951 in New Jersey, currently lives and teaches in San Francisco. The loss of her lover serves as the basis of her poem in this collection. She is the mother of two young children.

ADA AHARONI, Ph.D., is active in BRIDGE, an organization of Jewish and Arab women whose goal is peace in the Middle East. She has taught literature at many universities in the United States and Israel, and currently lives in Haifa.

YEHUDA AMICHAI, Israel's leading poet, has an international reputation. *The Selected Poetry of Yehuda Amichai*, edited and translated by Chana Bloch and Stephen Mitchell, was published by Harper & Row in 1986.

MERLE BACHMAN is a writer who also studies American Sign Language and dances whenever she can.

HAMUTAL BAR-YOSEF teaches Hebrew literature at Ben-Gurion University of the Negev. She has published four volumes of poetry and articles on literary criticism.

LEORA BAUMGARTEN is presently studying for her Ph.D. in Cellular Biology at the University of Chicago. An American who speaks Hebrew, she feels the language has had strong impact on her use of English.

RUTH BEKER lives in Israel and has been published in *Voices in the Ark: The Modern Jewish Poets*. She was born in Vienna, lived in Seattle, Wash., and moved to Israel in 1961.

SHARONA BEN-TOV is working on a second book of poems and will be Writer-in-Residence at Mishkenot Sha'ananim Colony in Jerusalem during 1990. In addition to her volume *During Ceasefire*, Harper & Row, 1985, her work has appeared in *The Paris Review*, *Harvard Magazine*, *Parnassus*, *The Yale Review*, and *Prairie Schooner*. Among others, her awards include the Bernard F. Connors Prize from *The Paris Review*. She has recently finished her Ph.D. in Modern Thought and Literature at Stanford University.

ALICE GLARDEN BRAND is Assistant Professor and Director of Composition at S.U.N.Y. College at Brockport, New York. In addition to her latest book of poems, *Studies on Zone*, BkMk Press, University of Missouri/Kansas City, 1989, she has published two scholarly works, *Therapy in Writing*, D.C. Heath, and *The Psychology of Writing: The Affective Experience*, Greenwood Press, 1989.

CARYL BULMER served on Israeli medical teams treating eye diseases in developing countries from Iran to Paraguay. She is the editor of *Seven Gates*, a multilingual journal of poetry and the arts published in Jerusalem, and has broadcast both poetry and fiction on the BBC.

SHULAMITH CAINE teaches at Drexel University, as well as in the Poets in the Schools program of the Pennsylvania Council on the Arts. Her work has appeared in *The American Poetry Review* and other publications.

MICHAEL CASTRO is the author of three books of poetry and of the critical study *Interpreting the Indian: 20th Century Poets and the Native American*. His poems appear in *Voices within the Ark: The Modern Jewish Poets*, *The Nuke Chronicles*, and recently in the *Tampa Review*. Castro is a senior editor of *River Styx Magazine* in St. Louis, Mo.

STANLEY F. CHYET is Director of the Magnin School of Graduate Studies at Hebrew Union College, Los Angeles. Together with Warren Bargad, he has co-edited *Israeli Poetry: A Contemporary Anthology*, Indiana University Press, 1986.

NANCY DATAN held academic positions in Illinois, West Virginia, Wisconsin, and in Israel, where she lived from 1963 to 1973. Her research on the problems of transition to middle age of Israeli women, *A Time to Reap*, was nominated for a National Jewish Book Award. Her essays have appeared in many magazines and collections, including *The Woman Who Lost Her Names: Selected Writings by American Jewish Women*. Harper & Row, 1980. She died in 1987 at the age of 46.

LUCILLE DAY is a science writer and education specialist in the Public Information Department at the Lawrence Livermore Laboratory, University of California at Berkeley. Her first collection, *Self-Portrait with Hand Microscope*, received the Joseph Henry Jackson Award.

SUSAN DICKMAN is a student at the University of California at Irvine, where she is working on an M.F.A. degree in Writing and in English.

MOSHE DOR was born in Tel Aviv and has published over twenty books. He has been Distinguished Writer-in-Residence at the American University, Washington, D.C. Since 1958 he has been on the editorial board of *Ma'ariv*, one of Israel's most important newspapers. In 1987 he received the Bialik Prize for *On Top of the Cliff: Selected Poems: 1954–1986*, and was elected president of the Israeli Chapter of PEN.

DINA ELENBOGEN is a native Chicagoan who lives in the city and teaches at Roosevelt and Loyola universities. Her work has appeared in *Midstream*, the *Chicago Times*, and *The Jewish Ledger*.

FLORENCE ELON has taught as a visiting poet at Northwestern and Yale universities and currently teaches Creative Writing at George Washington University. Her poems have appeared in *The Atlantic Monthly*, *The New Yorker*, *The Times Literary Supplement*, and *The Paris Review*.

ROBERT ESHMAN is a native of Los Angeles, Calif., and a graduate of Dartmouth College. He spent two years in Israel working as a freelance journalist. In Los Angeles, he served as West Coast Director of Friends of Peace Now (*Shalom Ach'shav*). He is currently at work on his second novel as well as on a translation of the works of Israeli poet Sami Shalom Chetrit.

RUTH FAINLIGHT has lived in London most of her life. She has published several poetry collections, the most recent being *Selected Poems*, Hutchinson, London, 1987.

MARCIA FALK's most recent book is *The Song of Songs: Love Lyrics from the Bible*, Harper & Row, 1989. She is currently writing *The Book of Blessings: A Feminist-Jewish Reconstruction of Prayer*, new liturgies in Hebrew and English, with essays, Harper & Row, 1991. A volume of Falk's translations of the Yiddish poet Malka Heifetz Tussman is being published by Wayne State University Press. Falk's translation of a poem by Zelda appears in this anthology. She teaches at Stanford University.

KINERETH GENSLER is a poetry instructor at the Radcliffe Seminars. Her two books of poems, *Without Roof* and *Threesome Poems*, were published by Alice James Books. She has been a Fellow at the MacDowell Colony and at the Ragdale Foundation. She spent her high school years in Jerusalem and returns there every year.

DAVID GERSHATOR, an American poet, was born on Mt. Carmel in Israel. He received a Ph.D. in Comparative Literature from New York University and has taught at several colleges, including the College of the Virgin Islands. His translations, reviews, and poetry have appeared in many publications. In 1983 New Directions published his edition and translation of *Federico García Lorca: Selected Letters*.

HAIM GOURI was born in Israel in 1923, fought with the Palmach in the war for Israel's independence, studied at the Sorbonne, had a career in journalism, and served as an officer in the Israeli Reserves. His first novel, *The Chocolate Deal*, 1965, is a Beckett-like allegory of absurdity in postwar Berlin. He has published more than a half-dozen collections of verse.

CAROL GREENBERG has been living in Israel since 1975. She has been a mother, grandmother, fashion designer, painter, and poet.

MIRIAM GROSMAN grew up in Berkeley, the child of Hungarian Jews who survived the Holocaust. Currently she is a resident of Mendocino, Calif., where she is involved in producing the Annual Mendocino Coast Jewish Film Festival and in developing her creative talents.

KATHRYN HELLERSTEIN's two books, which are translated editions of Yiddish poems by Moyshe-Leyb Halpern and Kadya Molodowsky, will soon be published. She has translated poems by Malka Heifetz Tussman and Yankev Glatshteyn in *American Yiddish Poetry*, University of California Press, 1986. Currently she lives in Philadelphia and is working on a book about Yiddish women poets.

ADINA HOFFMAN is a student at Wesleyan University. She received the Academy of American Poets Prize and is now writing a novel. She has lived in many places, including Houston, New Hampshire, and Jerusalem.

BARBARA HOLENDER is a native of Buffalo, New York, who has taught for the New York State Poets in the Schools program. She has published in many journals and newspapers and is included in *The New York Times Book of Verse*, Macmillan, 1970.

JOAN ZIA KAHN was recently married and is living in Beer Sheva, Israel, with her husband and young son, Yair. She received an M.S. in Management from Boston University, and has completed her studies at Ben Gurion University of the Negev.

TOBEY KAPLAN, originally from New York City, has lived near San Francisco for over ten years and has given readings in both cities. She currently conducts creative writing workshops at a county detention facility in the

Bay Area. She also works through Project Second Chance and coordinates the literacy program for inmates.

ELLIE HENKIND KATZ has a Ph.D. in psychology and teaches courses in personality development and psychotherapeutic avenues for change at Hebrew University. The mother of four, she is married to sculptor Michael Katz.

SHIRLEY KAUFMAN is an American poet living in Israel. In 1969 *The Floor Keeps Turning* won her an award from the International Poetry Forum. In addition to writing her own poetry she has translated works by the late Abba Kovner and by Amir Gilboa, among others. Her recent poems in *Claims*, Sheep Meadow Press, New York, 1984, show her concern for the Arab population of Israel.

SHARON KESSLER was born in Brooklyn in 1957. She attended the State University of New York at Binghamton and then Stanford University, where she was a Mirrielees Scholar in Literature and Creative Writing. In 1981 she made *aliyah* to Israel. She is the author of a book of poems, *The Insistence of Names*. One of her translations appears in this anthology.

IRENA KLEPFISZ is the author of *Keeper of Accounts*, 1983, and co-editor of *The Tribe of Dina: A Jewish Women's Anthology*, 1986, both published by Sinister Wisdom Books. An activist in both the Jewish and lesbian/feminist communities, she lectures, writes, and leads workshops on feminism, homophobia, Jewish identity, and anti-Semitism. In 1988 she received a National Endowment for the Arts Fellowship in poetry.

ABBA KOVNER was one of the commanders in the Vilna ghetto and a leader of the Partisans who were responsible for bringing thousands of Jews to Israel. In 1970 he was awarded the Israel Prize and was elected chairman of the Hebrew Writers' Association. His poems are haunted by symbolic visions that tie the Holocaust to the 1967 War. He died in 1987.

ESTELLE LEONTIEF has been the *Partisan Review* associate editor for fiction and poetry for over 15 years. *Genia and Wassily: A Russian Memoir* was published by Zephyr Press, 1983.

JONATHAN MAGONET is a rabbi, co-editor of the prayer books of the British Reform Synagogues, and Principal of Leo Baeck College, the Rabbinical Seminary of the British Reform and Liberal Movements. His anthology, *A Jewish Guide to the Here and Hereafter*, co-edited with Lionel Blue, will soon appear in the U.S. He lives in London.

SEYMOUR MAYNE has divided his time between Canada and Israel for the past twelve years. He has published *The Impossible Promised Land: Poems New and Selected*, and *Children of Abel*. One of his books, *Vanguard of Dreams*, has appeared in Hebrew and another is scheduled to be published soon. Mayne is on the Faculty of Arts at the University of Ottawa, Canada.

BERT MEYERS worked at many trades, including picture-framing, gilding, and teaching. His earlier works were published by Swallow Press, Double-day, Kayak, and more recently his work appeared in *Voices Within the Ark: The Modern Jewish Poets*, Avon Books, 1980. He died in 1979 at the age of 51.

RICHARD MICHELSON, the owner of an art gallery, lives in Amherst, Mass., with his wife and children. His book *Tap Dancing for the Relatives* was published by University Presses of Florida, 1985.

JO MILGROM received her Ph.D. in Theology and the Arts from the Graduate Theological Union, Berkeley, California, where she teaches. In her workshops artists study the roots of Jewish symbols, and experience the metaphors of the Bible through the study of text together with imaginative exercises.

RIVKA MIRIAM was born in Jerusalem in 1952. Her father was the Yiddish writer Leib Rochman. Her first book appeared when she was 14. She has published six books of poetry, one book of short stories, and one book of children's stories. She is also a painter and has exhibited her work in Israel and abroad.

JO-ANN MORT's poems, articles, and reviews have appeared in *Stand, Social Text, Midstream, Dissent, The Nation*, and *Commonweal*. She was assistant editor of *Pequod* where she was responsible for a special issue on Israel. She lives in New York City where she is the communications director of the Amalgamated Clothing and Textile Workers Union.

ALICIA OSTRIKER is the author of six volumes of poetry, including *A Woman Under the Surface*, Princeton University Press, and *The Imaginary Lover*, which won the 1986 William Carlos Williams Award. She is also the author of *Vision and Verse in William Blake*, and editor of Blake's *Complete Poems*. Her writing on women poets includes *Writing Like a Woman*, University of Michigan Press.

LINDA PASTAN has six books to her credit and has won several awards. *PM/AM: New & Selected Poems*, W. W. Norton & Co., 1982, was nominated for the

American Book Award. She has also taught at American University as well as at the Bread Loaf Writers' Conference. She lives in Maryland.

EDMUND PENNANT's work has appeared in many Jewish-interest and literary journals. He is a recipient of the Alfred Kreymborg Prize and the Mary Carolyn Davies Prize of the Poetry Society of America. He has published three collections of poems.

GABRIEL PREIL, originally from Estonia, has lived in New York since 1922. He is recognized as one of the leading Hebrew poets. He has been awarded many literary prizes, among them the New York University Neumann Award for lifetime achievement in Hebrew Literature. In 1975 he received an honorary doctorate from Hebrew Union College. In addition to Hebrew he has published in Yiddish. His ninth book, *Forty Poems*, is forthcoming.

DAHLIA RAVIKOVITCH, born in Israel in 1936, is the recipient of many Israeli literary awards. She has written five volumes of poetry and one of prose. Her most recent volume of poetry is *The Window: New and Selected Poems*, Sheep Meadow Press, 1989. Her poem "Wind-Up Doll" has become well-known abroad, not only for its feminist stance but also for its condemnation of indifference in the face of human subjugation.

ASHER REICH was recently awarded the Israeli Prime Minister's Prize for creativity. He has co-edited *Moznaim*, a literary monthly published by the Hebrew Writers Association, and has been cultural affairs editor of *Bamahane*, the Israel Defense Force magazine. For his eight volumes of poetry and a number of short stories, he has received numerous awards, among them the Israeli Publishers Prize, 1987. He was chosen to represent Israel at the International Writing Program of the Iowa Writers' Workshop in 1985.

ADRIENNE RICH is a major American poet who has been awarded the first annual Ruth Lilly Poetry Prize and a Brandeis University Creative Arts Medal. She teaches at Stanford University. Her most recent volume of poetry is *Time's Power: Poems 1985–1988*, W. W. Norton & Co., 1989.

STEVE ROOD is a lawyer in Oakland, California, who writes poetry.

JOEL ROSENBERG's poems, translations, fiction, and essays have appeared in *Ploughshares*, *Fiction*, and *Tikkun*. He is the author of a work of literary criticism, *King and Kin: Political Allegory in the Hebrew Bible*, Indiana University Press, 1986, and is a contributor to *The Literary Guide to the Bible*, Harvard University Press, 1987. He holds a doctorate in The History of Consciousness and teaches Hebrew and European Literature at Tufts University.

ANTHONY RUDOLF was born in 1942 in London, where he lives. A former editor of *European Judaism*, he has co-edited with Howard Schwartz *Voices Within the Ark: The Modern Jewish Poets*, Avon Books, 1980. He has also translated works by Russian and French poets. Currently he runs the Menard Press, whose books include a series of Hebrew poets in translation and publications on nuclear issues.

GRACE SCHULMAN has been the poetry editor of *The Nation* since 1972 and was the director of the Poetry Center at the 92nd Street YM/YWHA from 1974 to 1984. In addition to her poetry collections, *Hemispheres* and *Burn Down the Icons*, she is the author of several critical studies, among them *Marianne Moore: The Poetry of Engagement*, University of Illinois Press, 1987, and the editor of *Ezra Pound: a Collection of Criticism*, McGraw-Hill, 1974.

KARL SHAPIRO has been writing for more than half a century. During the 1950s he edited the Chicago periodical *Poetry*. In addition to his poetry, for which he won a Pulitzer Prize, he has written many critical essays, including *In Defense of Ignorance*, 1960. He is currently teaching in Davis, Calif.

REVA SHARON made *aliyah* in October 1987. Her poems have been published widely in anthologies and journals in the United States and Israel. Her book, *Pool of the Morning Wind*, was published in Israel in 1989. She has received grants from the Tel Aviv Foundation for Literature and Art and from the Women's League of Israel.

JAY SHIR grew up in Canada and South America and emigrated to Israel in 1973, after working as a composer and conductor of theatre music in Boston and Montreal. He is a former lecturer at Ben-Gurion University and an active small press magazine editor in Israel. He appears as a bass-baritone with the Jerusalem Chamber Opera. Currently he is associate editor of the *Tel Aviv Review*.

LAYLE SILBERT, a photographer of writers as well as a writer, has published in over thirty literary magazines. One of her poems was displayed in busses in New York State. Her book *Making a Baby in Union Park, Chicago* was published by the Downtown Poets in 1983.

ARYEH SIVAN was one of the founders of Hebrew literary magazines in the 1950s, including *Likrat*. He has also contributed regularly to *Ach'shav*.

MYRA SKLAREW has taught at American University in Washington, D.C., for 17 years. She is the author of six poetry collections, winner of the Alice di Castagnola Award from the Poetry Society of America, 1972, has been the director of Yaddo Colony in New York, and is poetry editor of *Lilith*.

E. M. SOLOWEY, the mother of six children, lives with her husband on Kibbutz Ketura where she does feasibility studies for famine prevention and for relief organizations. She has done research on crop introduction and arid lands orchardry for Ben Gurion University.

MARIE SYRKIN was a Professor Emeritus of Humanities at Brandeis University. She was editor of *Jewish Frontier* for many years. Her work includes *Golda Meir: Israel's Leader*; *Blessed is the Match*; *Your School, Your Children*; *Gleanings: A Diary in Verse*, a volume of original verse; and *The State of the Jews*, 1980. She died in 1989 at the age of 93.

AVITAL TALMOR was born in 1953 in Israel and grew up on a kibbutz. She spent two years in England where she became familiar with English literature, which became her passion, culminating with a postgraduate degree from the University of London. She now works for an insurance company and devotes her free time to writing. A collection of her poems will be published in England.

MADELINE TIGER has received numerous awards, among them the New Jersey State Council on the Arts Fellowship for Creative Writing, and a Fellowship in Writing, Columbia University School of the Arts. In addition to her poetry published by Fairleigh Dickinson University, she has co-authored *Creative Writing: A Manual for Teachers*, and has appeared in many anthologies and magazines.

RACHEL FARCHI UZIEL, born in Israel, has lived most of her life in Jerusalem. In addition to poetry, she has written children's stories and radio plays, one of which was produced at the Acre Festival in 1981. Her poems have appeared in *Seven Gates*, *Proza*, and *Ariel*.

JULIA VINOGRAD, known as the Berkeley Street Poet and Bubble Lady, has lived in Berkeley, California for 20 years and has 25 chapbooks of poetry reflecting her experiences. *The Book of Jerusalem* was a winner of the 1985 American Book Award of the Before Columbus Foundation. She holds an M.F.A. from the Iowa Writers' Workshop.

MORRIE WARSHAWSKI is a free-lance writer and media-arts consultant based in San Francisco. His work appears in such diverse publications as *The Wall Street Journal*, *San Francisco Examiner*, *American Film*, and *New York Quarterly*.

THEODORE WEISS has been writing poems and teaching literature and creative writing for over forty years. A collection of his life work, *From Princeton One Autumn Afternoon: Collected Poems of Theodore Weiss, 1950–1986*, was published by Macmillan in 1987. He has taught at many colleges, is the recipient of many awards, and together with his wife, Renee, edits and publishes the *Quarterly Review of Literature*.

RUTH WHITMAN is the author of six books of poetry, the most recent of which is *The Testing of Hanna Senesh*, Wayne State University Press, 1986. She has been a Senior Fulbright Writer-in-Residence at the Hebrew University in Jerusalem and won a Rhode Island Council on the Arts Grant in Literature. At present she is lecturer in poetry at Radcliffe College.

MEIR WIESELTIER was born in Moscow and emigrated to Israel as a child. He has published eight collections of poems as well as a selection of translations from English, French, and Russian. He works as poetry editor of the publishing house *Am Oved* in Tel Aviv.

NATAN ZACH arrived in Israel at the age of five from Berlin. An innovative use of dramatic immediacy typifies his work. He is also well-known as a political activist.

ZELDA (Schneurson Mishkovsky), an orthodox Jew from a line of Hassidic rabbis, was educated in religious girls' schools. Her first book of poems was awarded the Brenner Prize for Literature. Later publications earned the Bialik Prize. Her six volumes of Hebrew verse were reissued in 1985 as a collected edition, *The Poems of Zelda*, Kibbutz Hameuchad, Tel Aviv. Her mystical-religious sensibility has captivated a wide audience of non-religious readers in Israel.

CHAYYM ZELDIS, a novelist as well as a poet, has won wide critical acclaim for *Brothers*, Random House, 1976. He has won awards for both fiction and poetry and has contributed to *Accent*, *Commentary*, *The New York Times*, *The Milwaukee Journal*, and other publications. He spent nine years living on various agricultural settlements in Israel and has recently moved there.

LINDA ZISQUIT, born in Buffalo, New York, is a graduate of Tufts and Harvard universities, as well as of the writing program at the State University of New York, Buffalo. She is currently living in Israel with her husband and five children. She writes, translates, and teaches. She is looking for a publisher for her manuscript *Ritual Bath*. Several of her translations are included in this anthology.

Translators

KAREN ALKALAY-GUT: translator of Asher Reich's "Haifa in Winter." She is a professor of English at Tel Aviv University.

CHANA BLOCH: translator of Yehuda Amichai's "A Pace Like That"; CHANA BLOCH and ARIEL BLOCH: co-translators of Dahlia Ravikovitch's "The Horns of Hittin." CHANA BLOCH, the Chair of the English Department at Mills College, is a poet and a well-known translator of Hebrew poetry. ARIEL BLOCH is a professor at the University of California at Berkeley whose specialties are Semitic linguistics and Arabic dialects.

STANLEY F. CHYET and WARREN BARGAD: co-translators of Yehuda Amichai's "Laments on the War Dead": Haim Gouri's "Gehazi Visions"; Abba Kovner's "The Hour's Late" and "Sun-Watchers"; Dahlia Ravikovitch's "War's End"; and Natan Zach's "Prologue to a Poem." STANLEY F. CHYET's biography is listed among the contributors to this collection. WARREN BARGAD is Director of the Center for Jewish Studies at the University of Florida, Gainesville.

MARCIA FALK: translator of Zelda's "Pause." Her biography is listed among the contributors to this collection.

ROBERT FRIEND: translator of Gabriel Preil's "From Jerusalem, a First Poem." In 1950 Friend settled in Israel, where he taught English and American Literature for many years. His poems are widely published, as are his numerous translations of Hebrew poets.

BARBARA GOLDBERG: translator of Moshe Dor's "Crossing the River" and "Excavations." She is a recent winner of the Camden Poetry Award.

BARBARA and BENJAMIN HARSHAV: translators of "My Mother Died on Shavuot." BARBARA HARSHAV is a free-lance translator and Senior Associate Editor of the *Tel Aviv Review*. BENJAMIN HARSHAV is a professor of Hebrew in the Department of Comparative Literature at Yale University.

SHARON KESSLER: translator of Rachel Farchi Uziel's "Desecration of the Sabbath." Her biography is listed among the contributors to this collection.

GABRIEL LEVIN: translator of Meir Wieseltier's "Moving Lights." His poems and translations have appeared in many collections.

YISHAI TOBIN: translator of Hamutal Bar-Yosef's "Cry Sheep." He is a professor of linguistics at Ben-Gurion University and the author of several books.

LINDA ZISQUIT: translator of Yehuda Amichai's "Love of the Land"; Rivka Miriam's "Fastening the Light of the Sabbath Candles"; Dahlia Ravikovitch's "Stones"; and Aryeh Sivan's "To Live in the Land of Israel." Her biography is listed among the contributors to this collection.

Credits

DANNIE ABSE: "Of Two Languages" appeared in *Quarterly Review of Literature*, Poetry Series VIII, Vol. XXVII, reprinted by permission of the author.

NITZA AGAM: "Remaining Anonymous" from *State of Peace: The Women Speak*, Gull Books, 1987, reprinted by permission of the author.

ADA AHARONI: "The Second Exodus" from *From the Pyramids to Mount Carmel*, reprinted by permission of the author.

YEHUDA AMICHAI: "A Pace Like That" appeared in the original Hebrew in *The Hour of Grace*, used by permission of the translator Chana Bloch; "How Beautiful Are Thy Tents," "I Have Filtered Out," and "When a Man Has Been Away" from *Time*, Harper & Row, 1979, reprinted by permission of the publisher; "Laments on the War Dead" translated by Warren Bargad and Stanley F. Chyet from *Israeli Poetry: A Contemporary Anthology*, Indiana University Press, 1986, reprinted by permission of the publisher; "Love of the Land" appeared in *Ariel*, No. 71/72, 1988, reprinted by permission of the translator Linda Zisquit; "My Mother Died on Shavuot" appeared in *The Tel Aviv Review*, Vol. 1, 1988, reprinted by permission of the translators Barbara and Benjamin Harshav.

MERLE BACHMAN: "Even Through the Stone" printed by permission of the author.

HAMUTAL BAR-YOSEF: "Cry, Sheep" appeared in *Poetry Newsletter*, Fall 1984, reprinted by permission of the translator Yishai Tobin.

LEORA BAUMGARTEN: "The Land and I" printed by permission of the author.

RUTH BEKER: "No Pockets for Children" appeared in *The Literary Review*, Winter 1983, Vol. 26, No. 2, Fairleigh Dickinson University, reprinted by permission of the author.

SHARONA BEN-TOV: "Clouds over Jerusalem, in Winter" appeared in *The Paris Review*, Spring 1990, reprinted by permission of the author.

ALICE GLARDEN BRAND: "Subduing the Nile" appeared in *Dreaming of Wings: Women's Poems for Peace*, Poets & Peace International, 1984, reprinted by permission of the author.

CARYL BULMER: "Yamit" appeared in *Voices Israel*, 1983, reprinted by permission of the author.

SHULAMITH CAINE: "Ibn Gabirol in Tel Aviv" printed by permission of the author.

MICHAEL CASTRO: "Hear O Israel, O Palestine" printed by permission of the author.

STANLEY F. CHYET: "Sukkot in Jerusalem 5743" printed by permission of the author.

NANCY DATAN: "On Ordering Dog Tags" printed by permission of the author.

LUCILLE DAY: "Near Kibbutz Nir David" printed by permission of the author.

SUSAN DICKMAN: "In Wadi Ara" printed by permission of the author.

MOSHE DOR: "Crossing the River" and "Excavations" printed by permission of Moshe Dor and translator Barbara Goldberg.

DINA ELENBOGEN: "Apples of the Earth" appeared in *Seven Gates*, Jerusalem, Spring 1986, reprinted by permission of the author; "Maalot Cafe 9:00 A.M.," printed by permission of the author.

FLORENCE ELON: "Akbar" from *Treble Parts*, edited by D. T. Enright, London, 1975, reprinted by permission of the author.

ROBERT ESHMAN: "Acts of Loving Kindness" printed by permission of the author.

RUTH FAINLIGHT: "The Mount of Olives" from *Fifteen to Infinity*, Hutchinson, London, 1983, published in the U.S. by Carnegie-Mellon University Press, 1986, reprinted by permission of the author.

MARCIA FALK: "Dead Sea" from *This Year in Jerusalem*, State Street Press, Brockport, New York, 1986, reprinted by permission of the author.

KINERETH GENSLER: "The Border" from *Without Roof*, Alice James Books, Cambridge, 1981, reprinted by permission of the author.

DAVID GERSHATOR: "Jerusalem" printed by permission of the author.

HAIM GOURI: "Gehazi Visions" translated by Warren Bargad and Stanley F. Chyet from "*Israeli Poetry: A Contemporary Anthology*, Indiana University Press, 1986, reprinted by permission of the publisher.

CAROL GREENBERG: "We Watch the Rain and Speak of Peace" printed by permission of the author.

MIRIAM GROSMAN: "Summer Morning—Netanya" printed by permission of the author.

KATHRYN HELLERSTEIN: "Poem About Men" printed by permission of the author.

ADINA HOFFMAN: "Arriving" printed by permission of the author.

BARBARA D. HOLENDER: "The Tank" printed by permission of the author.

JOAN ZIA KAHN: "The Lion Whose Mane I Groom" printed by permission of the author.

TOBEY KAPLAN: "The Field" printed by permission of the author.

ELLIE HENKIND KATZ: "A Child Is Sick in the Night" printed by permission of the author.

SHIRLEY KAUFMAN: "Meeting in Ramallah" from *Claims*, Sheep Meadow Press, New York, 1984, reprinted by permission of the author.

SHARON KESSLER: "Even Our Trees Fight" printed by permission of the author.

IRENA KLEPFISZ: "East Jerusalem, 1987: *Bet Shalom*" printed by permission of the author.

ABBA KOVNER: "The Hour's Late" and "Sun-Watchers" translated by Warren Bargad and Stanley F. Chyet, from *Israeli Poetry: A Contemporary Anthology*, Indiana University Press, 1986, reprinted by permission of the publisher.

177

ANTHONY RUDOLF: "Ashkelon" from *After the Dream*, Cauldron Press, St. Louis, 1980, reprinted by permission of the author.

GRACE SCHULMAN: "Jerusalem Street Talk" from *Hemispheres*, Sheep Meadow Press, New York, reprinted by permission of the author.

LEAH SCHWEITZER: "A Rally for Peace" printed by permission of the author.

KARL SHAPIRO: "Israel" from *Poems 1940–1953* and from *Collected Poems, 1940–1978*, Random House, New York, 1978, reprinted by permission of the author.

REVA SHARON: "Covenant" from *Pool of the Morning Wind*, Shemesh Publishers, Jerusalem, 1989, reprinted by permission of the author.

JAY SHIR: "Safad into Night" printed by permission of the author.

LAYLE SILBERT: "Belonging" appeared in *The Jewish Frontier*, May 1985, reprinted by permission of the author.

ARYEH SIVAN: "To Live in the Land of Israel" appeared in *Ariel*, No. 71/72, 1988, reprinted by permission of Aryeh Sivan and translator Linda Zisquit.

MYRA SKLAREW: "At the Syrian Border" from *Altamira*, Washington Writers' Publishing House, Washington, D.C., 1987, reprinted by permission of the author.

E. M. SOLOWEY: "Winter Interlude" and "The Woman and the Sound of the Wind," printed by permission of the author.

ELAINE STARKMAN: "In the Kibbutz Laundry" from *Coming Together*, Sheer Press, 1977, and "Without a Single Answer" from *Beyond This Body*, Sheer Press, 1987, reprinted by permission of the author.

MARIE SYRKIN: "Protest Meeting" from *Gleanings: A Diary in Verse*, Rhythms Press, Santa Barbara, 1979, reprinted by permission of the author.

AVITAL TALMOR: "Historical Boomerang" printed by permission of the author.

MADELINE TIGER: "Your Hand" printed by permission of the author.

RACHEL FARCHI UZIEL: "Desecration of the Sabbath" appeared in *Proza*, May 1983, reprinted by permission of Rachel Farchi Uziel and translator Sharon Kessler.

JULIA VINOGRAD: "The Calling of Jerusalem" from *The Book of Jerusalem*, Bench Press, San Francisco, 1984, reprinted by permission of the author.

THEODORE WEISS: "The Here and Now" from *From Princeton One Autumn Afternoon: Collected Poems of Theodore Weiss, 1950–1986*, Macmillan, New York, 1987, reprinted by permission of the author.

RUTH WHITMAN: "Maria Olt" from *Permanent Address: New Poems 1973–1980*, Alice James Books, 1980, reprinted by permission of the author.

MEIR WIESELTIER: "Moving Lights" printed by permission of Meir Wieseltier and translator Gabriel Levin.

Index